# Standing Bear's Quest for Freedom

## The First Civil Rights Victory for Native Americans

LAWRENCE A. DWYER

*Foreword to the Bison Books edition by Judi M. gaiashkibos*

University of Nebraska Press ► Lincoln

*Betty Davis, 1934–2018*

In February 2009 Betty Davis called and invited me to give the keynote address at the 130th Anniversary celebration of the Trial of Standing Bear sponsored by the Douglas County Historical Society. At the time Betty was executive director of the Historical Society and I was a member of the board of directors. My research for that talk fired a passion within me to write the story of the trial of Standing Bear from a lawyer's perspective. The impetus to write this book would not have occurred without Betty's invitation, along with the insights and encouragement she generously gave to me, even within a month of her death. For that reason I dedicate this book to my dear friend Betty Davis.

## BEFORE WE CAME—THEY WERE HERE

Before the Declaration of Independence was signed and
the Constitution enacted—
**they were here.**
Before Lewis and Clark came—
**they were here.**
Before our ancestors came to live here—
**the ancestors of Standing Bear were here.**
Before we came, the Poncas—
hunted deer and buffalo,
fished for carp and trout,
planted and harvested corn, beans, and squash,
built their own homes
married and lived in family units,
educated their children,
defended their land,
supported themselves,
healed their sick,
honored their elders,
buried their dead,
remembered past glories,
and dreamed dreams.
**Before we came the Poncas were—**
living their own way of life—in a manner of their own choosing,
under their own rules for self-governance,
under their own system of law.
And then we came—
bringing a new system of law.
**And the two systems of law collided.**

# CONTENTS

# ILLUSTRATIONS

# FOREWORD

Judi M. gaiashkibos

I am deeply honored to be a small part of this excellent book. Lawrence Dwyer brings clarity and light to a story that has been at the center of my life.

As a Ponca woman, the forced removal of my relatives from their homeland in 1877 and the subsequent events leading to the trial of Chief Standing Bear in 1879 are deeply personal. For me these past events continue to remain a source of pain, pride, and inspiration. They are a call to action.

I am a descendant of the Ponca Chief Smoke Maker, *Shu-de-ga-xe*. My ancestor was painted by both Karl Bodmer and George Catlin, when each of these men separately spent time in the Ponca village. He signed several of the treaties between the United States and the Ponca. As a young man Standing Bear knew Smoke Maker, who was his elder. They shared similar qualities as men and as leaders.

The history presented in this book by my friend, author Lawrence Dwyer, is my history, but it is also our shared history, yours and mine. This story is not unique. Unfortunately, it is one of hundreds involving broken treaties, land grabs, and treatment of Indians as subhuman. My fellow Americans are quite unfamiliar with most of these stories because this history is not mainstream and not something that is taught in school.

*Standing Bear's Quest for Freedom* is written from a lawyer's perspective. It describes in documents and prose the moving events that led to the trial *Standing Bear v. General Crook*. There is much to admire and appreciate in the masterful and simple way this story is told. As a Ponca, I found many elements of the book that resonated with me, but here are a few highlights of the book that particularly struck me and I know will similarly be relatable for readers.

The author strives to tell this story in the words of the people who lived it. In this he succeeds brilliantly. A history involving the law, government policy, treaties, and the military could so easily get mired in technical language. This book never does. Rather, it maintains a crystal clarity, nimbleness, and focus on what matters, the people, their humanity and what happened before, during and after the courtroom.

Lawrence Dwyer introduces valuable context, the vanishing buffalo and the strategy behind it, an explanation of the writ of habeas corpus, which was the basic of Standing Bear's plea, and the treaties between the Ponca and the United States.

The trial is presented clearly and logically, including the witness testimony of Standing Bear, the closing arguments of Andrew Jackson Poppleton questioning the legality of the government's actions, Standing Bear's historic speech, and the court's decision.

Throughout the book the author takes special care to describe the cast of characters who lived this story. He describes how the court case came to be, connecting the activism of Thomas Tibbles, the deputy editor of the Omaha Herald, the conscience of General George Crook, and the actions of Chief Iron Eye of the Omaha Tribe and his daughter, Susette LaFlesche, Bright Eyes, who became Standing Bear's translator in the trial.

The Omaha were cousins to the Ponca and were horrified by what was done to their relatives. The Omaha father and daughter visited the commander of the Platte Region, General Crook. He "was so disturbed by what he heard from Bright Eyes and Iron Eye: He called Tibbles and things began to happen behind the scenes that would lead to the case based on the human rights of Native Americans that had never been recognized by United States law."

One of my favorite passages frames the response of Omaha citizens: "But for the courage, commitment, and kindness of a small group of people, this story would have had a very different and unfavorable ending for Standing Bear and his companions." And "they came together because in their heart they knew a terrible wrong had been committed."

There is a real sense that stars aligned in this moment. I particularly appreciated the detailed portraits of the distinguished legal team. The author further notes "the people of Omaha who packed the courtroom for the trial, cheered the ruling, and organized the Ponca Relief Committee." Finally, in a simple line, the writer says what is most true: "But there was only one leading man—One Hero!" It was indeed Standing Bear himself who awakened this response. His courage, his eloquence and nobility, led to the actions and sentiments of the Omaha community.

The writer proceeds in his narrative like an attorney presenting his case. Counselor Dwyer paints a portrait of the law and the humanity in this drama.

The author is an effective yet transparent storyteller. His book is both a labor of love and an achievement of research. His discoveries are relevant and helpful and provide just the right amount of information to create a flow moving forward.

As the book was being finished in 2019, a sculpture of Chief Standing Bear by Benjamin Victor representing the state of Nebraska was welcomed by Speaker Nancy Pelosi into Statuary Hall at the United States Capitol. This author captured what the sculptor also did. He showed us what it must have felt like to be in that courtroom in 1879 when a man stood up and reached out his hand to the world.

Standing Bear is a hero to me. I am so grateful to my friend Larry Dwyer for bringing this history to life in such a real and vibrant way. Larry has created a vivid picture of the events before, during, and after the trial and has never lost sight of the story's true hero, Standing Bear.

# PREFACE

This was a case of "firsts." For the first time in American history, a lawyer stood in a federal courtroom representing a client who was a Native American. A client who was not a "person" in the eyes of the law. A client who was not a "citizen" in the eyes of the law.

This was a case of "first impression," meaning it had no precedent for lawyers or judges. It had never been done before in a federal courtroom anywhere in America.

Chief Standing Bear was not a free man. It had been eighteen months since the government forcibly moved him and his fellow Poncas from their homeland near the Niobrara River to Indian Territory (present-day Oklahoma).[1] Standing Bear described what it was like for the Poncas to live in Indian Territory:

> Like a great house with a big fire in it, everything was poison. We never saw such kind of sickness before. One hundred and fifty of our people have died, and more are dying every day. It is the worst country in the world . . . there is no land there which will raise anything, and we have nothing to farm with, for they never brought us the things they took away. We had nothing to do but sit still, be sick, starve and die.[2]

Then, in December 1878, Standing Bear's teenage son, Bear Shield, died. In his final words, Bear Shield asked his father to take him home to be buried alongside the bones of his ancestors. The Poncas believed that if they were not buried with the bones of their ancestors, they would wander the next world alone. Family and tradition meant everything to the Poncas. Standing Bear, a loving father, promised his son he would take him home.

On January 2, 1879, a few days after Bear Shield's death, hungry, sick, and facing death themselves, Standing Bear and twenty-nine men, women, and children left the government-designated Indian Territory to return home. Standing Bear's quest for freedom had begun. All he ever wanted was the right to live and die with his family on his own land—on the beloved land of his Ponca ancestors—a free man.

Sixty-two days later Standing Bear and his companions arrived near Decatur, Nebraska, at the village of their cousins, the Omaha Tribe. Iron Eye (Francis LaFlesche), chief of the Omaha Tribe, and his daughter Bright Eyes (Susette LaFlesche) aided them with food, clothing, and medical care after seeing their awful condition—frostbite, bleeding feet, gauntness, torn clothing, crying children. The Poncas were sick, malnourished, and exhausted.

Three weeks later Gen. George Crook, commander of the Department of the Platte, received an order from his superiors to arrest these Poncas for leaving Indian Territory without government permission. The soldiers came to the Omaha Tribe's reservation and escorted them to Fort Omaha.

A terrible wrong had been committed against Standing Bear and the Poncas that needed to be corrected. Some compassionate and dedicated people in the city of Omaha, including newspaper reporter Thomas H. Tibbles and attorneys John L. Webster and Andrew J. Poppleton, devised a strategy to challenge the government's right to hold the Ponca prisoners against their will and to prevent them from being sent back to Indian Territory.

A trial of historic significance was held in Omaha, Nebraska, on May 1–2, 1879. It would have major implications for all Native Americans and their place in America and in the American legal system.

On May 12, 1879, federal judge Elmer S. Dundy issued a ruling that was unprecedented in American history. The first civil rights victory for Native Americans had been achieved. Standing Bear and his Ponca companions were declared to be "persons" under the law, free to leave their tribe and live independently, just as all other Americans. The atmosphere in the Omaha courtroom those first two days of May 1879 must have been electric. I can still feel it today.

*My Involvement*

American and British history was my major in college, yet the textbook used in a special course on the history of Nebraska, which I still possess, devotes only a few pages to the history of the Poncas.[3] Even in my three years of law school, the case was discussed sparingly.

My knowledge of this case was greatly enhanced in 2009, when I was a member of the board of directors of the Douglas County Historical Society, located in the Crook House on the grounds of the old Fort Omaha. Our board meetings took place in the dining room of the Crook House, across the hallway from General Crook's private office, still preserved today.

In May 2009 efforts were under way to commemorate the 130th anniversary of the Standing Bear trial via a series of events. Betty Davis, then executive director of the Douglas County Historical Society, requested that I make some remarks about the trial from a lawyer's perspective. On the day of the Society's commemoration of the trial, various presenters passionately shared information on Standing Bear from their diverse perspectives.

From that day forward I was encouraged to write a book from a lawyer's perspective. By this I mean, I prepared this book as would a lawyer researching and writing a brief for the court, relying on primary source material as much as possible and allowing the participants involved in the trial to speak for themselves. I included a background description of the events leading up to the trial and the impact the court's decision had on American law and culture.

The primary source materials I found included the four treaties the Poncas signed with the government, pertinent federal court decisions before and after the trial, government investigation reports, congressional legislation, ethnology studies, local and national newspaper accounts of the period, federal statutes, personal writings and briefs of the lawyers involved in the trial, books and letters written during that period, and much more, all in an effort to verify the facts as much as possible.

I was also able to locate a copy of the Application for Writ of Habeas Corpus written in John Webster's own handwriting and a copy of the brief of Andrew J. Poppleton written in his own handwriting. To read original pleadings and notes of these two respected lawyers in their own handwriting was especially inspirational to me since they did so without the use of a typewriter or computer. They were simply great lawyers and wordsmiths. Standing Bear could not have had better advocates.

I felt it was important in writing this book to interview judges and lawyers with knowledge of the case and federal court procedures to gather insights concerning the novel challenges and issues that the lawyers and the federal judge faced, and how they handled and decided them.

Early in my research I realized that the Poncas were a law-abiding people who had never broken a treaty with the government, had never taken up arms against the government, and were good neighbors to white settlers. They had their own system of law, with known rules of conduct enforced by a governing body. It was then that I wrote my poem, "Before We Came—They Were Here," to describe how the Ponca system of law collided with the American system of law, resulting in tragic consequences for the Poncas. This led to the focus of my book, *Standing Bear's Quest for Freedom*.

It all began because of the courageous leadership of one man, Standing Bear. He was an eloquent speaker and poet; a man of integrity, honor, and generosity. Above all he was a loving and devoted husband, father, grandfather, and friend. I feel very privileged to have spent ten years getting to know and appreciate this great man.

# Standing Bear's Quest for Freedom

# 1

## His Name Was Standing Bear

Among his people he was known as *Ma-chu-nah-zha*, sometimes written Ma-chu-na-zhi. Photographs taken near the time of the trial confirm the description that John G. Bourke, aide-de-camp to Gen. George Crook, wrote: "Standing Bear, the head man, was a noble looking Indian, tall and commanding in presence, dignified in manner; very elegantly dressed in the costume of his tribe."[1]

Standing Bear was an eloquent speaker. He could convey his inner feelings in poetic imagery and metaphors, leaving those who heard him mesmerized. To read his speeches, even today, nearly a century and a half later, is to feel his beautiful spirit and kind heart.

Growing up on the land of his ancestors near the Niobrara River within the Nebraska–South Dakota border, Standing Bear listened to his grandparents relate stories of the history and traditions of the Poncas. These stories enhanced the pride he carried in his heart for the bravery and determination his ancestors displayed as they defended their land, supported their families, and lived their way of life.

All Standing Bear ever wanted was to live and die on his own land.[2] He wanted to pass on these same stories to his grandchildren. It is how it had been done for generations. It was the Ponca way. This is a story of a great and noble man:

- A man who had been robbed of everything by the government, except his pride.
- A man whose heart was filled with love for his people and the land he called home.
- A man of courage, willing to travel five hundred miles in the cold and icy winter to bury his son in the ancestral burial grounds of the Poncas.
- A man determined to fight for his freedom as a human being.

*His name was Standing Bear.*

Fig. 1. Standing Bear with his wife, Susette Primo.
Courtesy History Nebraska, RG2066-05-022.

# 2

## Early History of the Poncas

In order to appreciate Standing Bear and his story, it is important to understand the historical background of his tribe. To trace the early history of the Poncas is to put together a puzzle. There is a "lack of archeological evidence in the form of a neat string of sites stretching back in time and space to the ancestral homeland of the Poncas; so we must rely upon other sorts of data in reconstructing the tribe's past," as pointed out by ethnologist James H. Howard.[1]

Published reports of the origin and customs of the Ponca Tribe by ethnologist James O. Dorsey suggest they were related to at least four other tribes—the Omaha, Osage, Kaw, and Quapaws, living somewhere "east of the Mississippi River."[2] Ethnologists Alice C. Fletcher and Francis LaFlesche (Woodworker) lived with the Ponca and Omaha Tribes and suggested their origins may have extended as far east as Virginia and North Carolina. Standing Bear said, "We have come back from the ocean, the great water to the East."[3]

### The Ponca Name

Early writings give different spellings of the Ponca name: Poncar, Puncahs, Pana, and Ponkas.[4] Eventually the Ponca, Omaha, Osage, Kaw, and Quapaw Tribes settled in the Ohio River Valley. In the early part of the sixteenth century, "some went down the Mississippi, hence arose their name 'Quapaw' meaning 'down-stream people,' the rest ascended the river taking the name 'U-ma-ha' (Omaha) meaning 'up-stream people.'"[5]

### Ancestral Land

After this separation in the sixteenth century, the Ponca and Omaha peoples followed the Missouri River upstream to Pipestone, Minnesota.[6] Because of the scarcity of buffalo and frequent attacks by the Dakota/Sioux, they separated again. The Omahas moved into northeastern Nebraska, and the Poncas settled in the Niobrara River valley on the border of present-day Nebraska and South Dakota.[7] Dorsey believed this final separation "must

Fig. 2. Alice C. Fletcher, Hartley Burr Alexander, Douglas Scott, Henry P. Eames, and Francis LaFlesche (woodworker), June 5, 1919. Courtesy History Nebraska, RG2026–73.

have occurred before 1673."[8] A map published in 1718 by cartographer Guillaume de l'Isle confirms these locations for the Ponca and Omaha tribes.[9]

### Horticultural People

The Poncas were a semisedentary horticultural people who treasured their ancestral land. The annual buffalo hunt provided them, as well as other Native American tribes, with nearly eighty different uses of the buffalo necessary for their survival.[10] Raymond J. DeMallie explains some of the uses: "Almost everything the Plains Indians owned, wore and used was made in part from the buffalo. Clothing, blankets, moccasin soles, tipi covers, ropes, containers, bags, saddles and glue were all made from buffalo hides, bones or hooves. Buffalo robes were the single irreplaceable source of most of the belongings of all Plains Indian peoples."[11]

The Poncas were such a family-oriented people that the hunters would make certain upon their return home from the hunt to take care of those members of the tribe who were elderly or otherwise unable to go on the hunt—they would "get the most tenderest meat."[12] They supplemented the annual buffalo hunt with corn, wheat, potatoes, squash, cabbage, onions, native plants, and fish caught in the Niobrara River.[13]

Soon they built earth lodges to provide a sense of permanence for their families. However, the close proximity of their homes within the village left them vulnerable to attacks by neighboring tribes, who could easily surround them. In addition, diseases, especially smallpox, brought by traders and other visitors could spread rapidly through their village.[14]

### Notable Visitors

Over the years, explorers, missionaries, traders (Spanish and French), mercantilists, and painters came to the Ponca villages. A few notable visitors from the nineteenth century left written memories of their time with them.

### Lewis and Clark (1804)

On September 5, 1804, in the early months of Lewis and Clark's two-year "Voyage of Discovery," William Clark visited the Ponca village and made the following entry in his journal:

> Set out early, the winds blew hard from the south as it has for some days past, we set up a jury mast & sailed, I saw a large gangue of turkeys, also grous seen . . . saw several wild goats on the cliff and deer with black tales. Sent Shields & Gibson to the Poncas Towns, which is situated on the Ponca River on the lower side about two miles from its mouth in an open butifull Plain, at this time this Nation is out hunting biffalow.[15]

Although Lewis and Clark never had a chance to sit down with the Ponca people, they estimated a population of about two hundred members, having been "reduced by smallpox and their war with the Soues."[16] Lewis and Clark separated after their historic journey. Meriwether Lewis died just a few years later in 1809. William Clark went on to a career in public service, including negotiating the first treaty between the United States and the Ponca Tribe in 1817. Later he was appointed superintendent of Indian affairs by President Monroe, with headquarters in St. Louis, Missouri. There he met George Catlin.

### George Catlin (1832)

After practicing law for a few years in his native Pennsylvania, Catlin went west with a strong desire to study the life and customs of the various Plains Indian Tribes and paint their portraits. Arriving in St. Louis in 1830, he met William Clark who took him on visits to tribes living near the Missouri River. Two years later Catlin boarded the American Fur Company's steamboat Yellowstone for a voyage up the Missouri River. He disembarked at the Ponca village to live with them for a few months.[17] The Ponca Tribe was very small when Catlin arrived, so he met most of the people, possibly including three-year-old Standing Bear.

In his journal, which accompanied his paintings, Catlin provides an eye-witness account of the life and customs of Standing Bear's people, noting they numbered less than five hundred, living in eighty earth lodges. He painted portraits of more than three hundred members of the various tribes he visited. He was especially drawn to Smoke Maker (Shu-de-ga-xe), chief of the Ponca Tribe, whom he painted wearing his full buffalo robe, saying: "He is a noble specimen of native dignity and philosophy. I conversed much with him, and from his dignified manners, as well as from the soundness of his reasoning, I became fully convinced that he deserved to be the sachem of a more numerous and prosperous tribe."[18]

### Prince Maximillian and Karl Bodner (1833)

Within a year of Catlin's visit, the renowned German explorer, ethnologist, and naturalist Maximillian, Prince Von Wied (1782–1867), visited the Ponca Tribe, accompanied by watercolor painter Karl Bodner of Switzerland. With the assistance of William Clark, they journeyed up the Missouri River and stayed in the Ponca village for a few weeks in May 1833.[19]

Prince Maximillian's diary of his journey, and many of Bodner's paintings of Native Americans, as well as some of George Catlin's paintings, are displayed in the Joslyn Art Museum, Omaha, Nebraska.

### Summary

The written records of these visitors describe a group of semisedentary horticultural people led by noble chiefs. The Poncas were the smallest tribe in the region. The government's 1780 census listed their population at 800.[20] In 1804 Lewis and Clark estimated their population at around 200.[21] Catlin estimated there were fewer than 500 members of the tribe when he visited them in 1832. At the time of their deportation to Indian Territory in 1877, the Poncas numbered 710. Somehow, despite their small size, various epidemic diseases, and attacks by neighboring tribes, the Poncas survived as a peaceful and honorable people, proud and determined to live and die on their own land.

# 3

## The Ponca System of Law

The Ponca Tribe developed a system of law based on their own customs and rules of conduct, evident in the way they governed themselves. The meaning of the term "law" in the American legal system was defined in *State v. Central Lumber Co.*, 123 N.W. 504 (S.D. 1909):

> The great and only excusable reason for the prescribing of any rule of conduct is to promote justice between man and his fellows in their relations as members of a social or political body. Law may be defined as the aggregate of those rules and principles of conduct promulgated by the legislative authority or established by local custom, and our laws are the resultant derived from a combination of the divine or moral laws, the laws of nature, and human experience.... The effort to promote and effectuate justice by means of human laws has been a continuous fight against human selfishness, especially human avarice and greed, a continual effort to protect the weak against the strong.[1]

According to this definition, the Ponca Tribe was a law-abiding, civilized people who promoted order, rules of conduct, and justice among its people.

### Permanent Lifestyle
The Poncas were a family-oriented people who nurtured their children and elders, and treasured the customs and traditions of their ancestors. Over time, they replaced tipis with permanent log cabins and supplemented the annual buffalo hunt with plantings of corn, wheat, squash, and potatoes.

### Rules of Conduct
In addition to their permanent lifestyle, the Poncas had clear rules of conduct for how their members were expected to behave. Tribal historian and interpreter Peter LeClaire was of Ponca descent and shared his own study, *Ponca History*, with ethnologist James Howard in 1949.

Howard said that LeClaire's "interesting document contains, in addition to the oral historical traditions of the tribe, a great deal of material on the customs, morals, and attitudes of the Ponca people of his own and earlier generations."[2]

Peter LeClaire summarized the seven basic principles that governed the rules of conduct for the Poncas:

1. Have one god
2. Do not kill one another
3. Do not steal from one another
4. Be kind to one another
5. Do not talk about each other
6. Do not be stingy
7. Have respect for the Sacred Pipe.[3]

### Tribal Organization

The Ponca Tribe was organized into kinship groups known as clans built along paternal bloodlines. Each clan was led by its own chief and had certain assigned duties for the overall benefit of the tribe.[4] At the time of the Standing Bear trial, there were nine clans.[5] White Eagle was the "Paramount Chief" of the tribe. Standing Bear was chief of the "Bear Clan." Photographs of Standing Bear often show him wearing a necklace of bear claws to signify his role in this clan and his position of tribal leadership.

The Ponca system of law was based on the simple philosophy that what was good for the tribe as a whole was of benefit for each member. The central governing body of chiefs encouraged a strong work ethic with tasks assigned to each clan, a common system of beliefs, individual accountability, and a desire to preserve and pass on their customs and traditions.

Ethnologist Alice C. Fletcher reported that the chiefs were responsible for "maintaining peace and order within the tribe, and making peace with other tribes."[6] Howard reported that the chiefs made their decisions in an effort "to act at all times in accordance with public opinion; complete, or nearly complete, unanimity was necessary before any action would be taken."[7] The members of the tribe used by the chiefs to enforce their decisions were known as the "Buffalo Police," because they were especially active during the buffalo hunts.

### The Sacred Pipe

The Sacred Pipe was an important instrument in Ponca society. When a member of the tribe broke a rule of conduct, the chiefs often assembled in a circle around the paramount chief as a sign of unity. They smoked the Sacred Pipe to allow the emotions of opposing parties to calm, and to allow the accused member an opportunity to speak for himself. The chiefs then arrived at a decision imposing an appropriate penalty.[8] For example:

- Punishment for thievery was either restitution[9] or whipping.[10]
- Punishment for adultery was often left to the injured spouse to decide.[11]
- Punishment for deliberate murder was usually banishment from the tribe for a number of years, unless the man was sooner forgiven by the relatives of the murdered man.[12]
- Punishment for disturbing the buffalo herd prior to the tribe's coordinated attack was whipping. Sometimes after the hunt was over and the offender had returned to the village with the rest of the tribe, the Buffalo Police would "give him gifts so that his heart would not be bad." In this way, the offender was "reincorporated into society."[13]

The correlation between breaking a rule of conduct and the penalty imposed reflected the Poncas' respect for each other and their desire to promote the common good of the tribe, seeking "conformity, not revenge."[14]

### Summary

The historical evidence supports the belief that prior to their forced removal in 1877 to Indian Territory, the Poncas lived and worked under their own system of law based on: (1) known rules of conduct for behavior; (2) organized clans with designated leaders and duties; (3) a council of chiefs who governed and employed the Buffalo Police to enforce their decisions; (4) a semisedentary lifestyle identified by permanent housing, horticultural plantings for food to supplement the annual buffalo hunt, and a strong family environment in which the members nurtured their children, respected their elders, and treasured the traditions and customs of their ancestors.

The Poncas were a law-abiding, civilized people desiring to be left alone to work their land in peace and to be buried alongside their beloved ancestors.

The government did not bring law and civilization to the Poncas, it brought its power and, eventually, the military.

# 4

## Precedents for the Ponca Removal in the American System of Law

As the government imposed its power and will upon the Poncas, the Ponca and American legal system collided. The Ponca system of law was simple and efficient. In stark contrast, the American system of law was a mixture of court rulings, congressional legislation, and treaties.

The precedent had been set during the nineteenth century for the forced removal of the Poncas from their ancestral homeland in 1877, through rulings of the United States Supreme Court and congressional legislation.

### Rulings of the United State Supreme Court

Two rulings of the United States Supreme Court in the early years of the nineteenth century had a disastrous effect on all Native Americans. First, the Court held that Native Americans were occupants of the land they lived on, not owners, under the "doctrine of discovery." Secondly, the Court ruled that Native Americans were not persons with rights and privileges under the American legal system, but were better described as "wards of the government."

### Doctrine of Discovery (1823)

The case of *Johnson and Graham's Lessee v. William M'Intosh*, 21 U.S. 543 (1823), came before the United States Supreme Court. The facts of the case are that private citizen Thomas Johnson "purchased" land in 1775 from a Native American tribe, the Piankeshaws. His descendants filed an action in the District Court of Illinois to eject William M'Intosh from "their" land. M'Intosh refused to leave alleging that he was the rightful owner holding a land patent from the federal government granted to him in 1818. Thus, two parties asserted ownership to the same tract of land, each claiming they had received title and ownership rights from different grantors: one grantor being a Native American tribe, and the other grantor being the United States government.

John Marshall, chief justice of the United States Supreme Court, affirmed the decision of the lower court in favor of M'Intosh, based in large part upon his interpretation of the "doctrine of discovery." This doctrine held that those European nations who discovered land in America took legal title to the land (ownership), subject only to the right of the Native Americans to occupy the land. Chief Justice Marshall wrote:

> They ["the original inhabitants"] were admitted to be the rightful occupants of the soil, with a legal as well as just claim to retain possession of it, and to use it according to their own discretion; *but* their rights to complete sovereignty, as independent nations, were necessarily diminished, and their power to dispose of the soil at their own will, to whomever they pleased, was denied by the original fundamental principle, that discovery gave exclusive title to those who made it.[1]

In support of his interpretation, Justice Marshall gave a detailed history of the various European nations who laid claim over centuries to land they discovered in America through "conquest" including Spain, France, Holland, and England. He concluded that "the history of America, from its discovery to the present day, proves, we think, the universal recognition of these principles."[2]

After the colonies defeated the British at Yorktown in 1781, Justice Marshall stated that the new United States government assumed the same right to ownership of all land that the European nations had previously claimed under the accepted "doctrine of discovery":

> By the treaty which concluded the war of our revolution, Great Britain relinquished all claim, not only to the government, but to the 'propriety and territorial rights of the United States,' whose boundaries were fixed in the second article. By this treaty, the powers of government, and the right to soil, which had previously been in Great Britain, passed definitively to these States. . . . *It has never been doubted*, that either the United States, or the several States, had a clear title to all the lands within the boundary lines described in the treaty, subject only to the Indian right

of occupancy, and that the exclusive power to extinguish that right was vested in that government which might constitutionally exercise it.[3]

Justice Marshall's interpretation of the "doctrine of discovery" would be challenged by John Webster in his closing argument in the Standing Bear trial fifty-six years later.[4]

### Wards of the Government (1831)

The Poncas, as well as other tribes, were deeply affected by a second major United States Supreme Court decision. In the case of *The Cherokee Nation v. The State of Georgia*, 30 U.S. 1 (Ga. 1831), Chief Justice Marshall held that Native Americans were like wards to a guardian:

They may, more correctly perhaps, be denominated domestic dependent nations. They occupy a territory to which *we assert a title independent of their will*, which must take effect in point of possession when their right of possession ceases. Meanwhile they are in a state of pupilage. Their relation to the United States resembles that of a ward to his guardian.[5]

In Chief Justice Marshall's reasoning, the powerful words of equality and freedom found in the Declaration of Independence did not include the original inhabitants of this land: "We hold these truths to be self-evident, that all men are created equal, that they are endowed by their creator with certain unalienable rights, that among these are life, liberty and the pursuit of happiness. That to secure these rights, governments are instituted among men, deriving their just powers from the consent of the governed."[6]

### Congressional Legislation

In addition to these two Supreme Court rulings, Congress enacted legislation in the nineteenth century that had adverse consequences for Native Americans.

### Bureau of Indian Affairs

In 1824 the Bureau of Indian Affairs was created under the jurisdiction of the War Department for the purpose of making treaties with various tribes. The Bureau's operations were transferred to the newly created Department of the Interior in 1849.[7] The intrusion into the life of the Poncas and other tribes by agents and inspectors of the Bureau was marked by unkept promises and long delays in delivering annuities, goods, and protection promised to them by the government in treaties.[8]

### Indian Removal Act

In 1830 Congress granted the president authority to negotiate treaties with Indian tribes for their removal to "Indian Territory"—present-day Oklahoma.[9] President Andrew Jackson expressed strong support for this legislation in a speech made to Congress a year later, in which he said it would be difficult for Native Americans to live too close to American citizens because:

> They have neither the intelligence, the industry, the moral habits, nor the desire of improvement which are essential to any favorable change in their condition. Established in the midst of another and a superior race, and without appreciating the causes of their inferiority or seeking to control them, they must necessarily yield to the force of circumstances and ere long disappear.[10]

Jackson didn't believe in entering into treaties with Native Americans either. In 1817, more than a decade before he was elected president, Jackson wrote a letter to then President James Monroe saying, "I have long viewed treaties with the Indians an absurdity not to be reconciled to the principles of our government. The Indians are the subjects of the United States."[11]

President Andrew Jackson's "Indian Policy" led to the removal of the Choctaw, Creek, Chickasaw, and Cherokee Tribes from their homelands in the southeast to Indian Territory during the 1830s. Their "Trail of Tears" led to the deaths of thousands of Native Americans. His policy set a precedent for the forced removal of the Poncas forty years later.

### Kansas-Nebraska Act

In 1854 Congress enacted the Kansas-Nebraska Act, which would change the landscape of American politics forever, eventually leading to a civil war. The issue of possible expansion of slavery into the Great Plains forced both the North and the South to encourage people to move into the area, since the issue would be decided by local vote, sometimes called "popular sovereignty." The lands belonging to Native Americans would suffer further confiscation by these new settlers. The issues presented by this act brought

Abraham Lincoln into the forefront of the national discussion, propelling him into the White House seven years later.[12]

### Homestead Act

In 1862 Congress promised to grant a free tract of land to anyone over twenty-one who had not taken up arms against the government, provided they made improvements to the land and stayed on it for five years.[13] Again, there would be more encroachment upon Native American land.

### Summary

As a result of these government actions, a massive influx of proslavery and antislavery activists, as well as homesteaders in search of a new life, came into the Nebraska Territory prior to and following the Civil War. They all had different motives for coming, but the result was the same: they encroached on tribal lands and disturbed the buffalo's natural habitat.

To promote and accommodate these new settlers, the government felt justified in moving some of the tribes onto smaller reservations and eventually to Indian Territory. The precedent for the government's action against the Poncas was set nearly a half-century earlier with the Supreme Court decision in the *Johnson* case (1823), the Supreme Court decision in the *Cherokee* case (1831), and the Indian Removal Act (1830).

Two principles were now firmly entrenched into the American legal system: (1) Native Americans had the right to possess the land they occupied, but the exclusive power to extinguish that right was vested in the government, independent of their will, under the "doctrine of discovery"; and (2) Native Americans were not persons or citizens in the eyes of the law, but were to be considered as "wards to their guardian," living under the perpetual protection of the government.

All Native American tribes, including the Poncas, could be moved from their homelands, at any time, to any place, at the will of the government.

**They were like pieces on a chessboard.**

# 5

## Treaties with the Poncas

In addition to Supreme Court rulings and congressional legislation, the American system of law included treaties made with Native American tribes. The Poncas signed four treaties with the government. The Poncas never broke a treaty; the government did. The guiding principle in dealing with Native American tribes after America won its independence was set forth in the Northwest Ordinance—act in good faith with the tribes. But often the government did not.

### The Northwest Ordinance (1787)

On July 13, 1787, the Continental Congress enacted the Northwest Ordinance for dealing with Native American tribes. The Ordinance said:

> The utmost good faith shall always be observed towards the Indians; *their lands and property shall never be taken from them without their consent*; and, in their property, rights, and liberty, they never shall be invaded or disturbed, unless in just and lawful wars authorized by Congress; but laws founded in justice and humanity, shall from time to time be made for preventing wrongs being done to them, and for preserving peace and friendship with them. (emphasis added)[1]

Attorney Charles E. Wright, in *Law at Little Big Horn*, wrote that, even before the English common law, good faith was the standard in all treaties and "applies to the negotiation, the agreement itself, and the manner in which the treaty is performed. It involves both action and intention. It is based entirely upon honesty, which is required of all parties to a treaty."[2] The Northwest Ordinance used absolute terms such as, "shall always" and "shall never," to declare its intent to respect Native Americans as owners of their own lands, not mere possessors.

### The United States Constitution (1789)

The United States Constitution continued the principle of good faith set out in the Northwest Ordinance, and established the paramount authority of any executed treaty in Article VI:

> *Article VI.* This constitution, and the laws of the United States which shall be made in pursuance thereof; and all treaties made, or which shall be made, the authority of the United States, shall be the supreme law of the land; and the judges in every state shall be bound thereby, anything in the Constitution or laws of any State to the contrary notwithstanding.[3]

The Constitution also provided a protocol for the three branches of government to follow in the treaty-making process, with its built-in delays that would prove difficult for the Poncas:

> *Executive Branch.* Article II. Section 2. gave sole authority for treaty-making to the executive branch of the Government stating that "the President shall have power, by and with the advice and consent of the Senate, to make treaties, provided two-thirds of the Senators present concur."[4]

> *Congressional Branch.* Article I. Section 8. stated that "the Congress shall have the power ... to regulate commerce with foreign nations, and among the several states, and with the Indian Tribes."[5]

> *Judicial Branch.* Article III. Section 2. stated that "the judicial power shall extend to all cases, in law and equity, arising under this Constitution, the laws of the United States, and treaties made."[6]

In 1801 Chief Justice Marshall, in his first year on the bench, wrote the opinion in which the Supreme Court affirmed the authority of the Constitution in this matter, holding in *United States v. Schooner Peggy* that "the constitution of the United States declares a treaty to be the supreme law of the land; of consequence its obligation on the courts of the United States must be admitted."[7]

The United States ratified 360 treaties with Native American tribes after the Constitution was enacted.[8] Four of these treaties were entered into with the Ponca Tribe: 1817, 1825, 1858, and 1865. Often the Poncas lacked a full understanding of what they were signing because many could not read or write English, and they often misunderstood the interpreters' explanations.

### The Ponca Treaty of 1817

The Poncas signed their first treaty with the government on June 25, 1817. Chief Smoke Maker, the same chief George Catlin painted and wrote about in 1832, was a signer. The government, represented by William Clark and Auguste Chouteau, initiated this first treaty because it wanted to establish a mutual relationship with the Poncas based upon "perpetual peace and friendship."[9]

### The Ponca Treaty of 1825

The Poncas signed their second treaty on June 9, 1825. Gen. Henry Atkinson and Maj. Benjamin O'Fallon signed on behalf of the government. The Atkinson-O'Fallon journal entry reported that as the parties came together in an open field, General Atkinson led his troops and musical band in a formal demonstration to show the power of the government, and his stature as its representative. After General Atkinson had spoken of the mutual peace and friendship between the parties, the Poncas signed the treaty and were given presidential medals. Nothing in the treaty had been negotiated with the Poncas. It had been written prior to the meeting by government representatives and simply presented to the Poncas for signature.[10] John Gale, a surgeon at Fort Atkinson and grandfather to Bright Eyes, signed the treaty as a witness. Chief Smoke Maker was again a signer on behalf of the Poncas.

This treaty was initiated by the government out of its desire to create a protocol for the Poncas to trade exclusively with licensed citizens of the United States, not with foreigners. The treaty stated: "All trade and intercourse with the Poncar tribe shall be transacted at such place or places as may be designated and pointed out by the President of the United States, through his agents; and none but American citizens, duly authorized by the United States, shall be admitted to trade or hold intercourse with said tribe of Indians."[11]

### The Ponca Treaty of 1858

On March 12, 1858, six chiefs representing the Ponca Tribe signed their third treaty with the government in Washington DC. The government was represented by Commissioner Charles E. Mix. The Poncas needed protection from Brule raids, and food rations because of serious crop failures.[12] The two main divisions of the Sioux Tribe were the Eastern Sioux (Dakota/

Santee) and the Western Sioux (Lakota). The Brule were one of seven sub-divisions of the Lakota.[13]

Facing starvation, the Poncas had only their land left to bargain with. The government acquired ninety-six thousand acres from the Poncas in exchange for four promises: (1) to protect their persons and property; (2) to make annuity payments staggered over thirty years; (3) to make a first-year payment of $20,000 to buy cattle and farming equipment, break up and fence the land, and build houses, "as may be necessary for their comfort and welfare;" and (4) to pay $5,000 per year for ten years to "build and maintain one or more manual-labor schools for the education and training of the Ponca youth in letters, agriculture, the mechanic arts, and housewifery."[14]

The Poncas were left with only thirty thousand acres of land after they signed this treaty.[15] The commissioner of Indian Affairs spoke of his real motive in treaty-making with the Poncas: "Treaties were entered into . . . with the Poncas . . . for the purpose of extinguishing their title to all the lands occupied and claimed by them, except small portions on which to colonize and domesticate them."[16]

### Difference in Timeline for Treaty Compliance

A major difference between the Ponca and American legal systems was in the timing of when promises made in a treaty would actually begin. The Poncas proceeded to carry out their obligations shortly after a treaty was signed by their chiefs. No other steps were needed to be taken and no one else had to be consulted. The chiefs had the final decision.

On the other hand, the government had to work through its slow procedural bureaucracy required by the Constitution from the time the treaty was signed by a representative of the president, followed by submission to the Senate for advice and consent. If the treaty was approved by a two-thirds vote of the Senate, the House would assign the treaty to a committee to determine what funds would be appropriated. When this process was completed, allocated funds would trickle down to the Bureau Agents for intended delivery to the Poncas, which was not always accomplished.

Shortly after the Treaty of 1858 was signed, the Poncas moved from their land and abandoned their growing crops. They expected the government to immediately protect them from Brule attacks and to fulfill their other treaty obligations. But the government did not. In the meantime, the Brule attacked the Poncas in late July 1859, killing some of their chiefs and other members of the tribe, destroying their tipis, stealing their horses, and doing considerable damage to their personal belongings. The Brule attacked again in September 1859. Yet the government failed to supply the Poncas with guns and ammunition to defend themselves, and failed to appropriate any of the promised annuity payments.

Government protection from the Brule attacks never came, in direct violation of Article 2 of the Treaty of 1858. The Poncas grew frustrated by the inaction of the government and discouraged by its broken promises. Yet the Poncas remained faithful to their treaty obligations.

### The Ponca Treaty of 1865

The Ponca chiefs signed their final treaty with the government on March 10, 1865, in Washington DC. The government delegation was led by Commissioner William P. Dole. Under the terms of this treaty, the Poncas ceded their remaining thirty thousand acres to the government in exchange for a return of the ninety-six thousand acres the government had acquired in the Treaty of 1858. The government said that it did this as a "way of rewarding them for their constant fidelity to the Government and citizens thereof, and with a view to returning to the said tribe of Ponca Indians their old burying grounds and corn fields."[17]

Unfortunately, Article 2 of the Treaty of 1865 imposed the following burden upon the Poncas, due to the success of the 1862 Homestead Act: "The United States shall not be called upon to satisfy or pay the claims of any settlers for improvements upon the lands above ceded to by the United States to the Poncas, but that the Ponca tribe of Indians shall, out of their own funds, and at their own expense, satisfy said claimants."[18]

### The Government's Blunder of 1868

On April 29, 1868, the government signed the Fort Laramie Treaty with the Lakota Sioux. In exchange for peace, the government gave the Lakota the western half of present-day South Dakota and, through a "clerical error" also gave the Lakotas the ninety-six thousand acres previously given to the Poncas in 1865. So, within three years, the government had given the same land to two different tribes![19] This Ponca land was located north of the Niobrara River and considered to be a crucial part of their ancestral land.

The ninety-six thousand acres were taken from the Poncas by the government without the Poncas' consent or knowledge, in direct violation of the Ponca Treaty of 1865 and Article VI of the United States Constitution. The Poncas received no compensation for this act of injustice. Historian Addison Sheldon called this "error" cruel, saying:

> It took away from them their home, their gardens, and the graves of their fathers, which they had defended against the Sioux for hundreds of years and made a present of them to their deadly foes, the Sioux. Nothing so cruel or unjust was ever done by the United States to another tribe of Indians. And this was done to a tribe which was always the friend of the white men. . . . The Poncas had no place to go and remained upon their old reserve even though in daily danger from the Sioux.[20]

Twelve years later, a congressional investigation confirmed the illegality of the government's action in unilaterally taking land from the Poncas:

> The committee have been unable to discover any reason for thus including this reservation within the Sioux reservation and thus depriving the Poncas of the land that had been before granted to them by the United States with a solemn covenant of warranty. The Commissioner of Indian Affairs, in his report for the year 1878, describes it as a blunder, in the following words: "by a blunder in making the Sioux treaty of 1868, the 96,000 acres belonging to the Poncas were ceded to the Sioux. The negotiators had no right whatever to make the cession."[21]

### Indian Appropriation Act (1871)

In 1871 Congress enacted the Indian Appropriation Act which stopped all treaty-making with Native American tribes, declaring: "Hereafter no Indian nation or tribe within the territory of the United States shall be acknowledged or recognized as an independent nation, tribe or power with whom the United States may contract by treaty; but no obligation of any treaty lawfully made and ratified with any such Indian Nation or tribe prior to March 3, 1871, shall be hereby invalidated or impaired."[22]

Ely S. Parker, commissioner of Indian Affairs at the time this act was enacted, supported the discontinuation of the treaty process, saying: "It is time that this idea should be dispelled, and the government cease the cruel farce of thus dealing with its helpless and ignorant ward."[23]

A startling statistic told the story of the effect the treaty process had on the Native American tribes. Native Americans went from owning all the land on the American continent to keeping just two hundred thousand square miles. On the other hand, the non-natives who once had no land on the continent now owned over three million square miles.[24] Professor Stan Hoig, in *White Man's Paper Trail*, wrote, "In the end, the United States won title to the Central Plains by military force, having often failed to do so legitimately on paper."[25]

### Summary

The government broke provisions of the treaties signed with the Poncas, including: (1) failure to protect them from the Brules; (2) failure to pay monies promised; and (3) in a cruel "blunder," giving ninety-six thousand acres sacred to the Poncas as traditional ancestral land to their rivals, the Sioux, which they had given back to them in treaty just three years earlier.

The Poncas and other Native American tribes were at a distinct disadvantage during the treaty-making process because of their general inability to speak, read, or write English, their misunderstandings of the interpreters' explanations, and the fact that the government representatives wrote all of the treaties. Rev. William H. Hare, Bishop of the Episcopal Church, who for many years ministered to the Poncas, confirmed their disadvantage in his testimony before the Senate Select Committee in 1880: "The Indians have no representatives who are competent to act for them . . . interpreters are too often very unreliable; and what they say with their mouth is often very different from what is written on the paper."[26] As treaty-making with the Poncas ended, the process of displacement began.

# 6

## The Ponca Displacement Begins

The government's policy of forced displacement of Native American tribes from their homeland was based in large part upon Supreme Court decisions, Congressional legislation, and broken treaties. The precedent had been established. Everything was now in place to move the Poncas from their ancestral homeland.

### Military Leadership

When Ulysses Grant was sworn in as the eighteenth president of the United States in March 1869, one of his first acts was to increase the presence of the military in the Great Plains by placing experienced Civil War generals in leadership positions. Gen. William Tecumseh Sherman was appointed general-in-chief of the United States Army. Lt. Gen. Philip Sheridan was placed in command of the military's Division of the Missouri, headquartered in Chicago. Within Sheridan's division, Brig. Gen. George Crook was appointed commander of the Department of the Platte, headquartered at Fort Omaha. By 1877 the military was in position to move the Ponca Tribe to Indian Territory.

### Vanishing Buffalo

At the same time, the buffalo herds, a staple for the Poncas and other tribes in the Great Plains, were vanishing. Killing the buffalo with rifles became a popular "sport" leading to the useless slaughtering of thousands of these animals, their carcasses left to rot in the sun. The government did nothing to stop this slaughter. Secretary of the Interior Delano commented in 1874: "The buffalo are disappearing rapidly, but not faster than I desire. I regard the destruction of such game as facilitating the policy of the government, of destroying their hunting habits, coercing them on reservations, and compelling them to begin to adopt the habits of civilization."[1]

General Sheridan also applauded the slaughter saying the white buffalo hunters "have done more in the last two years, and will do more in the next year, to settle the vexed Indian question, than the entire regular army has done in the last thirty years. They are destroying the Indian's commissary."[2]

It should be noted however, that "some military men, most notably General George Crook were known for their sincere concern for the Indians and their welfare."[3]

The inhumane slaughter of the buffalo caused terrible suffering for many of the Great Plains tribes who depended upon this special animal for its many uses vital to their survival. Ethnologist Alice C. Fletcher described the special songs and rituals that went into the annual buffalo hunt.[4] She said the slaughter of the buffalo also destroyed the hunt, which had a unique religious and social dimension to it: "The food on which their fathers had depended and which through past centuries had never failed, had been destroyed although they had been taught that the buffalo had been sent from every quarter for man's use, by Wakonda. Distress of mind accompanied their distress of body."[5]

### The Poncas Reach a Breaking Point

During the years between 1868 and 1876, in addition to the sufferings associated with the disappearance of the buffalo herds, the Poncas faced frequent attacks by the Brule, as well as everything nature could throw at them from drought to floods, and hailstorms to grasshoppers. Sometimes, all in the same year.

Rev. James Owen Dorsey, a missionary under the Indian Commission, stayed with the Poncas from May 1871 until August 1873 to study their language and culture. He made the following observations:

> From the time the snow disappeared until the snow came again, they were in constant fear of the inroads of the Brules. Several times while I was there, the Brules attacked the Poncas . . . In 1871 they planted and the Sioux came down and pulled up the corn. The Poncas replanted, and a part of the crop was injured by hail . . . In 1872, each head of a family had his piece of land laid off under cultivation and the crops were in fine condition, when the grass-hoppers came and destroyed about half. About two weeks later, there came a whirl-wind and hail-storm which destroyed nearly all the crops that remained.[6]

Dorsey greatly admired the spirit of the Poncas, writing: "They were very industrious and desirous of supporting themselves and their families . . . They lived in log-houses made by themselves, not at government expense; they were 18'x32', one story high, roofed with earth. There must have been in the neighborhood of two hundred . . . I could trust my property and my life with them."[7]

By 1873 the Poncas reached a breaking point when a great flood further damaged their land. At some point, the Poncas expressed the possibility that they might be open to moving onto the Omaha Tribe reservation, provided their cousins sold them land upon which to live and farm independently. Their openness to such a move changed in the summer of 1876, when the Poncas signed a peace treaty with the Brule.[8]

### Gold Discovered in the Black Hills

Prior to the Poncas' peace treaty with the Brule, the August 12, 1874, edition of the *Bismarck Tribune*, a newspaper in Dakota Territory, confirmed Gen. George A. Custer's report that he and a group of soldiers out on reconnaissance in the Black Hills had discovered "gold and silver in immense quantities."[9] The discovery was in a "mineral rich region of Western Dakota Territory that belonged to Sioux Indians according to the Fort Laramie Treaty of 1868."[10]

Prospectors soon entered the area to mine for gold, without consent of the Sioux. The government made little or no effort to keep them out, in violation of their obligations under the Fort Laramie Treaty of 1868. As settlers began to follow the prospectors into the area, the Sioux resolved to protect their land and way of life from this incursion. The Cheyenne joined them and defeated Custer's Seventh Cavalry Regiment at the Little Big Horn, June 25, 1876.[11]

In the spring of 1877, as a result of the defeat of Custer's regiment and the public outcry that followed, the government responded by moving the Northern Cheyenne to Indian Territory. At the same time the government moved the Poncas there as well. This decision was made even though the Poncas, unlike the Northern Cheyenne, had never taken up arms against the government. The Poncas had never broken a treaty with the government and were friendly neighbors to the settlers. There was no justification for the government to move the Poncas, except for the fact that it could because the Poncas were small in number and defenseless.[12]

The Bureau of Indian Affairs sent Inspector Edward C. Kemble to visit the Poncas and begin the process of displacement of the tribe from their homeland.

---

**Edward C. Kemble (1828–86)**

Edward Cleveland Kemble was born in 1828 in Troy, New York. As a teenager, he traveled to California to work for newspapers as printer and editor. He served as a sergeant in John C. Fremont's Bear Flag Revolt of 1846 against Mexico and later mined for gold. He became a correspondent for the Sacramento Union newspaper during the Civil War. His first visit to the Poncas was in 1862. He returned in 1872–73 representing the Episcopal church by supplying them with food and clothing, and even serving as a sponsor for some of the Ponca children at their baptisms. He died in 1886.[13]

---

### Kemble Suggests a Trip to Indian Territory

On January 26, 1877, Inspector Kemble arrived at the Ponca village to meet with their chiefs: Paramount Chief White Eagle, Standing Bear, Big Elk, Little Picker, Standing Buffalo, Sitting Bear, Little Chief, Smoke Maker, White Swan, and Lone Chief.

Kemble informed the chiefs that the government had decided to move the Ponca Tribe to Indian Territory.[14] The chiefs said they did not want to go. They wanted to stay on their own land. Standing Bear rose to speak on behalf of the chiefs, saying, "This is our land; we were born here. We have lived here all our lives. We are growing old here and we hope to die here."[15]

Inspector Kemble knew he had a difficult situation on his hands. He suggested the chiefs accompany him to Indian Territory to see the land reserved for them. He promised them that if they did not like it, they could meet with President Hayes at the White House.[16]

### Chiefs Visit Indian Territory with Kemble

On February 2, 1877, Kemble and the Ponca Chiefs drove wagons to Yankton, the capital of Dakota Territory, where they boarded the train for the five-hundred-mile journey to Indian Territory. They were accompanied by James Lawrence, Indian Affairs agent, Charles LeClaire, Indian Affairs interpreter, and Rev. Samuel D. Hinman, Episcopal minister. Kemble said that he took the Reverend Hinman along because "he has known the Poncas ever since his tribe, the Santee, for which he is the missionary, have settled on the river."[17]

At Independence City in southeastern Kansas, the group left the train and drove wagons the remaining distance to the Osage village in the northeast corner of Indian Territory. The Ponca chiefs immediately realized the land was not suitable for farming because it was dry, dusty, and laden with rocks. The hard soil was not good for growing corn, wheat, squash and potatoes. In addition, they could see that their cousins, the Osage and Kaw tribes, were sick and sad.[18]

Chief White Eagle described what he saw when they reached Indian Territory: "We were sick twice and we saw how the people of that land were, and we saw those stones and rocks and thought these two tribes [i.e., Osage and Kaw] were not able to do much for themselves."[19]

When the chiefs expressed their dislike of the areas visited, Kemble drove them thirty miles to Arkansas City, on the border of Indian Territory and Kansas. The chiefs had their picture taken at Bonsall's Studio on February 20, 1877, and stayed in the Central Avenue Hotel with Kemble. The February 21, 1877, edition of the *Arkansas City Traveler* published this report:

A party of eleven Ponca Indians from Dakota Territory arrived at this place on Saturday afternoon. They came via Independence, Kansas and visited the Osage and Kaw Agencies on their way, the whole time occupying eleven days. All are large and powerful men, and apparently intelligent. The Ponca tribe numbers 730 people, who have advanced considerable in farming and agricultural pursuits. They claim the Osage treated them very coldly, and reported the country they were going to see as bad land, so as to discourage them from coming.[20]

The chiefs had had enough. White Eagle spoke to Inspector Kemble, saying:

| | |
|---|---|
| **White Eagle:** | Take me with you to see the Great Father [the President]. You said formerly we could tell him whatever we saw, good or bad, and I wish to tell him. |
| **Kemble:** | No, I don't wish to take you to see him. |
| **White Eagle:** | If you will not take me to the Great Father, take me home to my own country. |

| Kemble: | No, I'll not take you to your house. Walk there if you want. |
|---|---|
| White Eagle: | It makes my heart feel sad, as I do not know this land.[21] |

In the morning, Kemble and his group left the hotel and boarded a train for Dakota. Kemble had no intention of fulfilling his promise. He gave the chiefs two choices: accept the land offered to them in Indian Territory or walk home. The chiefs refused to stay, but without any money or passes for a train ride, and with no horses or wagons, they decided to walk home, with only blankets for warmth.

The Ponca Chiefs walked on the railroad tracks when possible until they came to Wichita, Kansas where they tried to board a train offering their moccasins as barter. The depot attendant was willing to let them board the train until he received a telegram from Edward Kemble ordering him not to let them board any trains. So the chiefs continued walking home, living on raw corn given to them by white settlers, and sleeping among stacks of wheat to keep warm from the freezing nights. After fifty days they arrived at the Otoe Tribe reservation in southeast Nebraska. They were given food and horses, and after ten days were sent on their way. Five days later they arrived at the village of their cousins, the Omaha Tribe, sick and exhausted.[22]

On February 13, 1880, in Washington DC before the Senate Select Committee on the Ponca Removal, Bright Eyes gave a detailed description of her direct knowledge of the chiefs' story concerning what happened in Indian Territory and their journey to her village. She testified that her uncle, White Swan, who was one of the Ponca chiefs, stayed in her mother's home and told her what they had endured. Her father, Iron Eye, Chief of the Omaha Tribe, also heard their story. Bright Eyes further testified that when Standing Bear and the other chiefs came to dinner at her home, "they were all tired out and nearly sick. They were in really a pitiful condition. They stayed three or four days with me. Several other Omahas were present."[23]

### Telegram to President Hayes Goes Unanswered

After the chiefs told their story and were comforted by the hospitality of their cousins, they left on the last leg of their journey home. But first, they stopped in Sloan, Iowa, on March 27, 1877, to send a telegram to President Rutherford B. Hayes. Bright Eyes said, "I wrote the telegram for the Poncas; Mr. Hamilton copied it."[24] The chiefs asked the president a simple question:

Did you authorize the man you sent to take us down to the Indian Territory to select a place for our future home, to leave us there to find our
way back, as best we could, if we did not agree to go down there? This
he told us, and left us without a pass, interpreter, or money, because
we could not select one of three places, telling us if we did not go there
peaceably, we would be driven by soldiers, at the point of the bayonet,
from our present homes. We were so left and have been thirty days getting
back as far as the Omahas, hungry, tired, shoeless, footsore and sad of
heart. Please answer us at once, for we are in trouble.[25]

The telegram was signed by White Eagle, Standing Bear, Smoke Maker,
Standing Buffalo, Frank LaFlesche, Little Chief, Big Elk, and Gahega.[26] The
president did not reply. In her testimony before the Senate Select Committee, Bright Eyes stated that she was told this fact by White Eagle and by
her uncle White Swan.[27] After Bright Eyes testified to this, the committee
chair, Senator Dawes, inserted into the committee record the reply sent to
Kemble by the Indian Commissioner:

> Washington D.C. 3rd mo. 31, 1877
> To E.C. Kemble, Springfield, Dakota:
>
> Missing Ponca delegates reported at Omaha Agency 27th, whence
> they telegraphed to President for help to reach home. No aid will
> be furnished unless you direct.
>
> John Q. Smith,
> Commissioner[28]

An editorial that appeared in the March 31, 1877, edition of the *Sioux City
Journal* (of Sioux City, Iowa) expressed strong sympathy for the Poncas:

> From the communication published elsewhere, from the chiefs and the
> principal men of the Ponca Indians, it is evident that there is no longer
> any room for doubting that the proposed removal of this tribe from its
> home of two hundred years, to a new and comparatively barren section,
> is not to be accomplished without all possible resistance upon the part of
> its members. The charges they make are such as cannot be overlooked

by people who believe that Indians have rights which anybody is bound to respect. They have been grossly deceived in numerous ways, if not by the promises made to them by the agent of the government, at least in their comprehension of these promises . . . Put yourself in their place and see how you would like it.[29]

## Order of Removal

The chiefs arrived back in their village on the Nebraska-Dakota border on April 2, 1877. Inspector Kemble was waiting for them with an order from the newly appointed Secretary of the Interior, Carl Schurz, to move the Poncas to Indian Territory.

---

**Carl Schurz (1829–1906)**
President Rutherford B. Hayes appointed Carl Schurz as secretary of the interior in 1877 with the task of cleaning up the Bureau of Indian Affairs. Schurz was born in 1829 in Germany and came to American in 1852. He soon became active in the antislavery movement. He was appointed ambassador to Spain in 1861, but returned to fight in the battles of Chancellorsville and Gettysburg, rising to the rank of brigadier general. After the Civil War, he worked as a newspaper editor in Missouri where he was elected to the Senate. He died in New York on May 14, 1906.

---

## Standing Bear and Big Snake Arrested

When the chiefs were informed of Secretary Schurz's Order of Removal, they assembled in tribal council to decide how to respond. Standing Bear said they would not leave their land. He described what happened next:

Then the soldiers came, and we locked our doors, and the women and children hid in the woods. Then the soldiers drove all the people the other side of the river, but my brother Big Snake and I. We did not go; and the soldiers took us and carried us away to a fort [Fort Randall] and put us in jail. There were eight officers who held council with us after we got there. They kept us in jail ten days. Then they carried us back to our home. The soldiers collected all the women and children together; then they called all the chiefs together in council; and then they took wagons and went round and broke open the houses. When we came back from the council, we found the women and children surrounded by a guard of soldiers. We told them we would rather die than leave our lands; but we could not help ourselves. *They took us down.*[30]

### Removed without Free Consent

The Senate Select Committee Report of 1880 condemned the removal of this friendly and peaceful people from their ancestral land without their free consent:

> It is remarkable that never in the history of the Ponca tribe of Indians had the soldiers of the United States ever been called on to preserve the peace among them until this effort of E.C. Kemble to remove them from their old home under orders from the Indian Bureau based upon the law which required their free consent to their removal. Forty soldiers were brought from Fort Randall, and remained with them until the tribe finally left their homes for the Indian Territory . . . The removal of a tribe of Indians who had always been in friendly relations to the government from their homes on a reservation confirmed to them by solemn treaty to a distant, and to them unknown, section of country, was a matter of great importance, and worthy the earnest consideration in all its details of the head of the department. The first duty under the law was manifestly to obtain in some authentic manner the consent of the tribe of Indians to be removed.[31]

The Senate Report also chastised Inspector Kemble and his superiors at the Department of the Interior for the manner in which the entire removal process was handled:

> Kemble was called to this duty, and apparently without any knowledge as to his fitness. His instructions from time to time evidenced a lack of appreciation on the part of the Department of the dignity and importance of his work. With this most important matter in the hands of a person totally unfitted for the work devolved upon him, accompanied by indifference and lack of knowledge upon the part of his superiors, what follows is not only not surprising, but entirely inevitable. . . . At no time did those representing the government ever frankly and fairly state to

these Indians that they had the liberty of free choice to stay upon their own lands or to remove to the Indian Territory.[32]

## Summary

Without weapons, these peaceful, honorable Poncas had stood against the government with great courage and heartfelt resolve. But they were powerless against soldiers armed and ordered to move them south.

Almost everything they possessed—their homes, their land, their farm implements, their household goods, their very way of life—was about to be taken from them.

**Soon, what the Poncas had known and cherished would be gone.**

# 7

## Journey of Sorrows

In the spring of 1877, the government appointed E. A. Howard to replace Edward Kemble as inspector to the Poncas. In 1873, while in charge of the Spotted Tail Agency, Howard had been charged with fraud involving a beef requisition contract, but a government commission had exonerated him. The government then reassigned him to the Ponca Agency.[1]

Howard decided to hold one more meeting with the Ponca chiefs in an attempt to get them to voluntarily leave their land. On May 15, 1877, after four hours of unsuccessful talks, the soldiers began to carry out the order to forcefully remove the Ponca tribe from their homeland.[2]

### Ponca Property Destroyed

The Poncas were told to take everything they owned to the Indian Agency building before they left their homes. A few years later, in an interview with Thomas H. Tibbles, deputy editor for the *Omaha Daily Herald*, Standing Bear said that it took him three days to comply with the government order because he had accumulated so much property. Proud of his hard work, yet deeply saddened and disheartened, Standing Bear described the property the government took from him:

> One house (I built it with my own hands. It took me a long time for I didn't know how very well). It was twenty feet by forty feet, with two rooms, three lamps, four chairs, one table, two new bedstands, two washtubs and washboard, two new cooking stoves, one heating stove, two trunks (one very large), one valise, crockery, knives and forks. I also had four cows, three steers, eight horses, four hogs, five wagon-loads of corn with the side-boards on (about 130 bushels), one hundred sacks of wheat, and one wagon-load loose, which I had in boxes (about 275 bushels), twenty-one chickens, two turkeys, one prairie breaking plow, two stirring plows, a good stable and cattle sheds, three axes, two hatchets, one saw, three pitchforks, five plows, a good stable and cattle sheds, one cross-cut saw, two log chains, two ox-yokes, two ladders, and a great many other

things which I cannot now remember. These things were mine. I had worked for them all. By their order, I brought them all, except the house and such things as I could not move, to the Agency, and they put them in a big house and locked them up. I have never seen any of them since. Our wagons and ponies they did not take away.[3]

At a reception held in the home of Josiah Fiske in New York City two years later, it was reported that Standing Bear repeated these words about losing the house he built and added "now I live in a tent."[4]

Thomas Tibbles testified before the Senate Select Committee regarding what he saw when he visited the Ponca villages in the fall of 1879:

> The Ponca tribe consists of two bands: the one under White Eagle lived on the Niobrara River; the one under Standing Bear lived on the Missouri River. The Agency building, sawmill, blacksmith shop, etc. were on the Missouri River village. They were five miles apart. 29 houses were still standing. Part of Standing Bear's house was torn down to within four feet of the foundation, and all the materials of the upper part carried away. On the Niobrara side all the houses were torn down.[5]

Paramount Chief White Eagle confirmed Tibbles's testimony, saying that after the Poncas had left their Niobrara village, the soldiers tore down all of their log homes which the Poncas had built themselves mostly from logs or sawed lumber from the tribe's sawmill. The soldiers also tore down all their barns, cattle sheds, tribal grist mill, sawmill, schoolhouse and their church. The blacksmith shop and the Indian Agency building were left standing. Some fifty cooking stoves were broken into pieces. The logs from their homes were thrown into piles for auction.[6]

It must have looked like a tornado had ripped through the Ponca villages. Almost everything was gone; destroyed for no reason.

### Driven Like a Herd of Ponies

At the time of the removal there were 710 members in the Ponca tribe.[7] The Poncas were taken from their homeland in two groups.

The first group consisted of Lone Chief and 170 members; they left on April 17, 1877, for Indian Territory, escorted by Inspector Lawrence and a group of soldiers. Kemble joined them later and stayed with them until they arrived at the Quapaw reservation, June 12, 1877.

The second group of 540 men, women and children, including Standing Bear, left on May 16, 1877, escorted by Major Walker and 25 soldiers. They were joined by Inspector Howard.[8]

Chief White Eagle testified before the Senate Select Committee in 1880 that the women and children greatly feared the soldiers when they began the 1877 forced march: "They forced us across the Niobrara to the other side, just as one would drive a herd of ponies; and the soldiers pushed us on until we came to the Platte River. They drove us on in advance just as if we were a herd of ponies."[9]

### Howard's Diary of the Forced March

The terrible suffering and utter horrors experienced by the Ponca people on their forced march to Indian Territory, was described by Inspector E. A. Howard in his *Journal of the March*. As the government representative who accompanied Standing Bear's group of Poncas, he had firsthand knowledge of what could be called their Journey of Sorrows (also referred to as the Ponca Trail of Tears). Howard's *Journal* was included in the Annual Report given by the commissioner for Indian Affairs to the Secretary of the Interior for the year 1877. Included are the following excerpts from Howard's *Journal*:[10]

May 16. They [the Chiefs] sent word to me at an early hour that they had considered my words and had concluded to go with me, and that they wanted assistance in getting the old and infirm over the Niobrara River which was much swollen by the rains and at a low temperature. . . . At five o'clock p.m. had the entire tribe with their effects across the river, off the reservation, and in camp in Nebraska. . . . The current so swift that it was found impossible to move the goods across in any other way than by packing them on the shoulders of the men, the quicksand bottom rendering it unsafe to trust them on the backs of animals.

May 19. A severe thunderstorm occurred during the night of the 16th and heavy rains prevailed during the day and night of the 17th, rendering it impossible to make any further preparations for breaking camp. . . . For two or three hours before daybreak on the 19th it rained heavily. . . . During the day an Indian child died.

**May 23.** The morning opened with light rain, but at eight o'clock a terrific thunderstorm occurred of two hours' duration, which was followed by steady rain throughout the day, in consequence of which we remained in camp. During the day a child died.

**May 24.** Buried the child that died yesterday in the cemetery at Neligh, giving it a Christian burial.

*Note*: At the brief burial service for White Buffalo Girl, her father made a heartfelt plea to the people of Neligh to take care of the grave of his eighteen-month-old child as they would one of their own. The people of Neligh have honored his wishes to this day with flowers and toys laid at her tomb.[11]

**May 27.** The morning opened cold, with a misty rain. . . . Broke camp at eight and marched eight miles further down Shell Creek, when a heavy thunderstorm coming on, we again went into camp. Several of the Indians were here found to be quite sick, and having no physician, and none being attainable, they gave us much anxiety and no little trouble. The daughter of Standing Bear, one of the chiefs, was very low of consumption, and moving her with any degree of comfort was almost impossible . . . same trouble existed in transporting all the sick.

**May 28.** Last evening, I gave orders to break camp at 5:00 this morning, intending, if practicable, to reach Columbus before night, but a heavy thunderstorm prevailed at that hour.

*Note*: Bright Eyes said her uncle White Swan, a Ponca Chief, sent word to the Omahas that they should meet the Poncas near Columbus, Nebraska to say goodbye since they may never see their cousins again. She, her father Chief Iron Eye, and eight other Omahas rode over—"we met them on the road; they were all crying. I heard men crying all night."[12]

**June 6.** Prairie Flower, wife of Shines White, and daughter of Standing Bear, who died yesterday, was given Christian burial, her remains being deposited in the cemetery at Milford, Nebraska, a small village on the Blue River. Quite a heavy rain during the afternoon. The storm, the most disastrous of any that occurred during the removal of the Poncas under my charge, came suddenly upon us while in camp on the evening of this day. It was a storm such as I never before experienced. . . . The wind blew a fearful tornado, demolishing every tent in camp, and rending many of them into shreds, overturning wagons, and hurling wagon-boxes, camp-equipages, etc. through the air in every direction like straws. Some of the people were taken up by the wind and carried as much as three hundred yards. Several of the Indians were quite seriously hurt, and one child died the next day from injuries received.

**June 9.** Put the child that died yesterday in the coffin and sent it back to Milford, to be buried in the same grave with its aunt, Prairie Flower.

**June 16.** Reached Marysville, Kansas where we went into camp. During the march a wagon tipped over injuring a woman severely. Indians out of rations and feeling hostile.

**June 18.** Little Cottonwood died. Four families determined to return to Dakota. I was obliged to ride 9 miles on horseback to overtake them to restore harmony and settle difficulty in camp. Had coffin made for dead Indians. A fearful thunderstorm during the night, flooding the camp equipage.

**June 25.** Two old women died during the day.

**July 9.** Broke camp at six o'clock, passing through Baxter Springs at about one o'clock. Just after passing Box Springs, and between that place and the reservation, a terrible thunderstorm struck us. The wind blew a heavy gale and the rain fell in torrents, so that it was impossible to see more than four or five rods distant, thoroughly drenching every person and every article; making a fitting ending to a journey commenced by wading a river and thereafter encountering innumerable storms.

In his final journal entry Howard wrote: "During the last few days of the journey the weather was exceedingly hot, and the teams terribly annoyed and bitten by green-head flies, which attacked them in great numbers. Many of the teams were nearly exhausted and had the distance been a little farther, they must have given out. The people were all nearly worn out from the fatigue of the march."[13] Howard recorded in his *Journal* the deaths of nine members of the Ponca Tribe during the course of the fifty-five-day march: five children, two young adults, and two elderly women.

### The Poncas Arrive in Indian Territory

Howard was with the Poncas for a few days before the removal and remained with them in Indian Territory for a brief time. He then left them to fend for themselves, writing:

> I am of the opinion that the removal of the Poncas from the northern climate of Dakota to the southern climate of the Indian Territory, at the season of the year it was done, will prove a mistake, and that a great mortality will surely follow among the people when they shall have been here for a time and become poisoned with the malaria of the climate. It is a matter of astonishment to me that the government should have ordered the removal of the Ponca Indians to Indian Territory without having first made some provision for their settlement and comfort. As the case now is, no appropriation has been made by Congress; no houses have been built for their use, and the result is that these people have been placed on an uncultivated reservation to live in their tents as best they may.[14]

Howard acknowledged that the Poncas had not consented to the removal, saying: "The title to the old Ponca reservation in Dakota still remains in the Poncas, they having signed no papers relinquishing their title nor having violated any of the provisions of the treaty by which it was ceded to them by the government."[15]

In his testimony before the Senate Select Committee on the Removal of the Poncas in 1880, Standing Bear described what happened when the Poncas arrived in Indian Territory: "In our own land we lived in houses made of wood that kept out snow and rain and kept us warm in winter. Many of us had two stoves each to keep the house warm, but when we went down there we had to live in tents that let the rain and snow get in, and we had no stoves; and so a great many of my people got sick and died."[16]

The same Senate Report confirmed Standing Bear's testimony: "The Tribe was taken to the Indian Territory without any previous arrangement for their permanent location there. They were temporarily located near Baxter Springs, on the Quapaw reservation and lived in canvas tents during

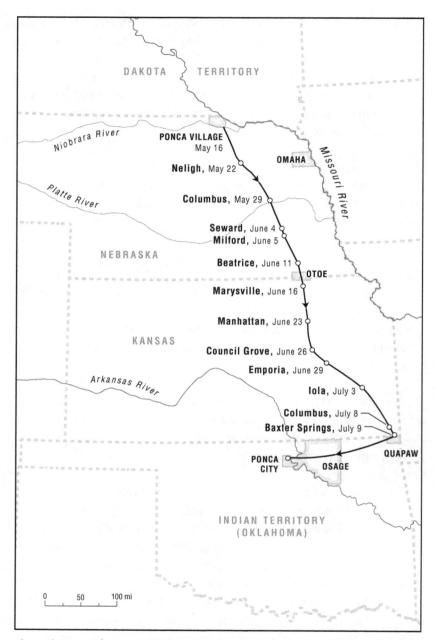

DAKOTA TERRITORY

Niobrara River

PONCA VILLAGE
May 16

OMAHA

Missouri River

Neligh, May 22

Columbus, May 29

Platte River

Seward, June 4
Milford, June 5

NEBRASKA

Beatrice, June 11
OTOE

Marysville, June 16

Manhattan, June 23

KANSAS

Council Grove, June 26

Arkansas River

Emporia, June 29

Iola, July 3

Columbus, July 8
Baxter Springs, July 9

QUAPAW

PONCA
CITY
OSAGE

INDIAN TERRITORY
(OKLAHOMA)

0    50    100 mi

Fig. 3. The Poncas' Journey of Sorrows, May 16, 1877–July 9, 1877. Locations and dates are from E. A. Howard's "Journal of the March."

the winter. . . . They became exceedingly home-sick and discontented, which aggravated greatly the evils under which they were suffering."[17]

### The Ponca Chiefs Meet President Hayes (1877)

Paramount Chief White Eagle and Chief Standing Bear requested a personal visit with the President. Secretary Schurz, upon the recommendation of the new Indian commissioner E. A. Hayt, granted their request. White Eagle, Standing Bear, and other Ponca chiefs boarded a train to Washington DC where they met with President Rutherford B. Hayes in early November 1877. The President told them to remain in Indian Territory, and assured them the government would take better care of them. While in Washington DC they posed for a group photo, and Standing Bear posed for an individual photo in his Chief's attire.

### The Chiefs Return to Indian Territory

When the chiefs returned to Indian Territory, they found their people in worse condition than when they had left. Standing Bear's sister, grandmother, and mother-in-law had died of fever and malnutrition. The Poncas had no means to support themselves. In less than eighteen months since their removal, a total of 158 of the original 710 members of the tribe died of pneumonia, malaria or malnutrition. Nearly one-fourth of the tribe was dead.[18]

At the Senate hearing in 1880, Chief White Eagle described what he saw when he returned: "Every person and animal was sick or dying. We were as grass that is trodden down." One committee member asked the chief a very direct question to which White Eagle gave just as direct an answer:

**Committee:**    Why do you not cultivate land down there?
**White Eagle:**    Our ponies died of disease; and our cattle died; and then we had no plows. That is the reason.[19]

That same Senate investigation issued a blunt assessment in its final report of the government's forced removal of the Ponca tribe made without their consent:

This failure had involved the government in a transaction which can find no justification. It has led the government to violate in dealing with one of the most peaceable, orderly and well-disposed of all the tribes of

Fig. 4. Ponca delegation who met President Hayes, Washington DC, November 1877. *Back:* John Barnaby *(left)* and Charles H. LeClaire (interpreters.). *Front (left to right):* Standing Bear, Paramount Chief White Eagle, Standing Buffalo, Big Elk. Courtesy History Nebraska, RG2066-04-02-1.

Indians, in the most flagrant manner, their rights of property, to disregard their appeals to the honor and justice of the United States, and the dictates of humanity. The Committee can find no language sufficiently strong in which to condemn the whole proceedings and trace to it all the troubles which have come upon the Poncas, and the hardships and sufferings which have followed them since they were taken by the United States from their old reservation and placed in their present location in the Indian Territory.[20]

## Summary

The Poncas had exhausted all attempts to get help from the government, even their direct appeal to the president failed. They were illegally removed by force from their land by the soldiers fulfilling government orders. Their homes, church and school were torn down. The Journey of Sorrows to Indian

Fig. 5. Standing Bear poses for a formal portrait during his visit with President Hayes, Washington DC, November 1877. Courtesy History Nebraska, RG1227-02-02.

Territory claimed nine lives, including the daughter of Standing Bear. Within a little more than a year, most of their ponies and 158 of their people were dead. Where could they turn for help?

The Poncas had no legal rights or standing in any federal court to file a petition for a redress of grievances or crimes committed against them, because the American legal system considered them merely "wards of the government," not persons.[21]

The Poncas could be arrested at any time for leaving their reservation in Indian Territory without government permission.

The government, at any time, could and did take away their land, homes, farm equipment, threshing machines, reapers, crops, buildings, and household furniture, without compensation or justification.

Sickness and death were their constant companion.

The Poncas' hope for survival was gone.

Something must be done.

Someone must take action.

# 8

## Standing Bear Takes Action

Within a year and a half after being forcibly taken from his ancestral home land and moved to Indian Territory, Standing Bear's daughter Prairie Flower, his sister, grandmother, and mother-in-law had all died. Now in December 1878 his teenage son, Bear Shield, died. His death was especially difficult for Standing Bear because his son had received an education in the Ponca village school and could speak English.[1] In the Ponca tradition, the oldest son would one day assume his father's position as a chief in the tribe.[2]

Bear Shield made a final request to his father to be buried alongside the bones of his ancestors in his homeland. It was a tradition that if a Ponca was not buried with the bones of his ancestors, he would wander the next world alone. Family and tradition meant everything to the Poncas. Standing Bear was a loving father, so he promised his son he would take him home and bury him in the ancestral burial grounds of his people. Later Standing Bear reflected on his decision to go home:

> I was in an awful place, and I was a prisoner there. I was not a free man. I had been taken by force from my own country to a strange land and was a captive. I could see nothing ahead but death for the whole tribe. I was much sorry for the little children who were so very sick. They would moan and moan, and we had no medicine and no way to help them. I said I will take a small party and start back to my old home. If the soldiers come after us I will not fight. Whatever they do, it can't be worse than to stay here.[3]

### Standing Bear Begins His Quest for Freedom

On January 2, 1879, facing hunger, sickness and death, with no recognized standing to file an action in any American court for protection or redress of grievances, Standing Bear left Indian Territory. Twenty-nine men, women and children left with him, including wife Susette, his two small grandchildren, children of his deceased daughter Prairie Flower, his brother Yellow Horse with his family, and Buffalo Chip, chief of the Medicine clan. Standing Bear carried with him the bones of Bear Shield.

Led by Standing Bear, these courageous Poncas left Indian Territory in four wagons and a few horses on a five-hundred-mile journey home. They rode out in a snowstorm facing below-zero temperatures and howling winds. All of their food and money was gone within twenty days.[4]

Enduring cold, ice, hunger, thirst, sickness, fear, and worry of the unknown, they must have wondered what they would face when they got home—if they ever reached home. The likelihood of some or all of them dying on the journey was real.

They might not have survived the journey but for the kindness of some white settlers along the way. Standing Bear recalled that "the white people treated us very kindly; some gave us bread, some coffee, and others meal or flour; none of them refused to give us anything when they saw we were hungry."[5] Such acts of kindness, together with Ponca resolve and Standing Bear's promise to his son, allowed them to push onward toward home. But what would await them?

Lt. John G. Bourke, aide-de-camp to General Crook, remarked that Standing Bear and his companions set out from Indian Territory "at their own expense across country, walking every foot of the way, molesting nobody, and subsisting upon charity. Not a shot was fired at anyone; not so much as a dog was stolen."[6]

## March 4, 1879

Sixty-two days into their journey, Standing Bear and his companions arrived at the village of their cousins, the Omaha Tribe. It was March 4, 1879. Chief Iron Eye (Joseph LaFlesche), Bright Eyes (Susette LaFlesche), and a few others heard of their arrival and went to greet them. They were shocked at what they saw. The Poncas were starving from malnutrition, their feet were bleeding, and frostbite had blackened their skin. The Omahas tended to their every need. They listened to them share their sad ordeal. They gave them land and seed to plant crops, and did everything possible to nurse them back to health and help restore their lives.

On the day the Poncas arrived at the Omaha reservation, Jacob Vore, Indian agent to the Omahas, sent a telegram to the office of Carl Schurz informing him that "the Poncas have just arrived thirty in number; had them arrested, they promise to remain for orders, have no place to confine them. I await instructions."[7]

Secretary Schurz then sent an order by telegram to George W. McCray, secretary of war, saying, "the nearest military commander be instructed to detail a sufficient guard to return these Poncas to the agency where they belong."[8]

McCray set the process of arrest in motion. First, on March 14, he transmitted Schurz's letter to General Sherman, who in turn forwarded the message to General Sheridan on March 17. Two days later Gen. George Crook, commanding general of the Department of the Platte, stationed at Fort Omaha, received his orders from Sheridan.[9]

General Crook directed John H. King, commander of the Ninth Infantry and post commander at Fort Omaha, to send a detachment to the Omaha tribal village near Decatur, Nebraska, to arrest the Poncas and escort them back to Fort Omaha.[10]

### Poncas Arrested

First Lt. William L. Carpenter, of the Ninth Infantry, together with a corporal and five enlisted men, using three saddle horses and a military ambulance drawn by four mules, was dispatched to the Omaha village. On March 23, 1879, the soldiers arrived there and arrested Standing Bear and the twenty-nine Poncas. A few of the Poncas were still not well enough to travel and were allowed to remain on the Omaha reservation.

Standing Bear described what happened: "When we started back the scene among the women and children was heart-rending. They and their friends among the Omahas cried most bitterly. It would break one's heart to look at them. Many were still sick, and all felt that we were going back to certain death. My efforts to save their lives had failed."[11]

Rev. James O. Dorsey, an eyewitness to their arrest, said: "I saw them leave today. Their appeals to me were touching. Said Standing Bear: 'My friend, you know us. We can't live down there where the Great Father put us. So we came here to live and work the land.'"[12]

Bright Eyes was also a witness to the arrest and feared the soldiers were taking the Poncas directly back to Indian Territory:

We were all formerly one people, the same as brothers. . . . Standing Bear said it was no use to resist, they had committed no crime, had done no wrong, but the government was strong, and they were powerless and could not resist. The next morning the soldiers started off with them; we were standing by the door and saw the whole company file past, as the soldiers were taking Standing Bear and his companions down to the Indian Territory. The Omahas felt very bad; but they could not even go and shake hands with them.[13]

---

**Chief Iron Eye (1818–88)**

Iron Eye (Joseph LaFlesche) was Native American and French. His mother was a Ponca (Watunna). For most of his life, he lived with the Omaha Tribe and succeeded Big Elk as Paramount Chief. He is considered to be the last chief of the Omaha Tribe. White Swan was his brother (or step-brother) and a Ponca chief, who kept Iron Eye and Bright Eyes informed of the Poncas' sufferings. Iron Eye firmly believed that his children should be educated and learn to speak English. For example, son Francis LaFlesche (Woodworker) became an ethnologist and authored books on the Omaha Tribe with Alice C. Fletcher. Daughter Susette (Bright Eyes) became the first Native American teacher in the tribe's school as well as a national figure in the Indian reform movement. Another daughter, Susan LaFlesche Picotte, became the first Native American physician.

---

*Summary*

Standing Bear had promised to take the bones of his son home to the Poncas' ancestral burial grounds in Nebraska. Even though he knew that any Ponca who left Indian Territory without government permission would be arrested, he set out for home anyway, accompanied by family and friends. They arrived at the Omaha reservation sick and exhausted.

The government issued an order for their arrest and return to Indian Territory, but due to their sick condition it was delayed. The Poncas had gained a reprieve for a few days if something, or someone, could come to their aid.

Fig. 6. Iron Eye (Joseph LaFlesche), Chief of the Omaha Tribe, 1854. Father of Bright Eyes. Courtesy History Nebraska, RG2026–01.

# 9

## Imprisoned at Fort Omaha

On March 27, 1879, Standing Bear and his fellow Ponca prisoners arrived at Fort Omaha, escorted by 1st Lt. William L. Carpenter and a contingent of the Ninth Infantry. The soldiers set up three temporary tent lodges near the entrance to the fort. The Poncas would remain there for fifty-four days.[1]

Commander John H. King sent a telegram to R. Williams, assistant adjutant general, saying, "several of the Indians are sick with chills and fever, and it will be necessary for the entire party to remain here a few days so that their ponies may recuperate sufficiently to enable them to proceed on their return to Indian Territory."[2]

### Fort Omaha

Fort Omaha was built by the government in 1868 on sixty acres, four miles north of Omaha, Nebraska. It was named Sherman Barracks in honor of Gen. William Tecumseh Sherman. Ten years later it was updated and renamed Fort Omaha. A modern home was added in 1878 for the commanding general, but not occupied by General Crook and his wife until the fall of 1879.[3] Former president Ulysses S. Grant and his wife visited the Crooks in November 1879 and stayed in their home for three days. In September 1880 President Rutherford B. Hayes dined at the Crook home.[4] Crook and Hayes were close friends from their days serving together during the Civil War.

*Note*: Today, the "Crook House" on the grounds of old Fort Omaha is open to the public and serves as headquarters for the Douglas County Historical Society.[5]

### Department of the Platte

The recently created Military Division of the Missouri, headquartered in Chicago, was under the command of Lt. Gen. Philip Sheridan. The Department of the Platte was created in 1866 as a military district within the Division of the Missouri to include present-day Iowa, Nebraska, Wyoming, Utah Territory, and parts of Montana and Idaho. The Department of the Platte was responsible for fourteen supply and administration posts in that region

Fig. 7. Crook House ("Quarters One") on the grounds of Fort Omaha. Courtesy Douglas County Historical Society.

and coordinated campaigns against various northern tribes. General Crook became commanding general of the Department of the Platte on April 27, 1875. He moved the department headquarters from the southwest corner of Fifteenth and Harney Streets in downtown Omaha, to Fort Omaha.[6]

### George Crook (1828–90)

George Crook was born on September 8, 1828, on a farm near Dayton, Ohio. He graduated from West Point in 1852, finishing thirty-eighth in a class of forty-three cadets. Crook fought at Manassas, Antietam, and Chickamauga as a cavalry leader and was present at Appomattox Courthouse when Lee surrendered to Grant. He served in the western theatre of operations after the war and was promoted to major general in 1873. In 1875 he assumed command of the Department of the Platte and moved to Omaha. His photographs proudly display his forked beard and the unusual hats he liked to wear when not in uniform (which was most of the time). He was an avid hunter and taxidermist, and loved to lift weights before breakfast. At the time of the Standing Bear trial he was fifty years old.[7]

Fig. 8. Staff officers of the Department of the Platte, 1878–79. General Crook (*seated, front row middle*), Judge Advocate Horace B. Burnham (*seated, front row far right*), Lt. John G. Bourke, aide-de-camp to General Crook and reporter at Crook interview of Ponca prisoners (*standing, third from left*). Courtesy Douglas County Historical Society.

## Omaha Tribe Fears Forced Removal

The Ponca and Omaha Tribes came together to the Nebraska/Dakota region a few hundred years earlier. They lived near each other and often intermarried. Chief Iron Eye and his daughter Bright Eyes were very close to their cousins, and had first-hand knowledge of the sufferings the Poncas had endured the past two years.

Now, in March 1879, the Omaha Tribe knew Standing Bear and his Ponca companions likely faced death as soon as the military could return them to Indian Territory. Chief Iron Eye, Bright Eyes, and the rest of the Omaha Tribe were awakened to the fact that what the government had done to the Poncas it could do to them as well.

Bright Eyes expressed her fear: "The Omahas have always been afraid, as far back as I can remember, that the government would take their lands away from them. When the land of the Poncas was taken from them, the Inspector told the Poncas . . . that the Omahas would be taken down to the Territory too, very soon. That scared the Omahas."[8]

Ethnologist Alice C. Fletcher, in her study of the Omaha Tribe, confirmed the fears of the Omaha tribe:

> Suddenly, in 1877, like a bolt out of the blue sky, came the distressing removal of their kindred, the Poncas, from their home on the Niobrara River to the Indian Territory. The pathetic return in the spring of 1879 of Standing Bear and his followers, bearing the bones of that chief's dearly loved son for burial, and the coming of United States soldiers to carry them back to the dreaded "hot country," brought terror to every Omaha family, thinking that their own homes might be in danger . . . and that even the government which they had always respected, had betrayed them.[9]

### Chief Iron Eye and Bright Eyes Visit General Crook

Sometime during the last week of March 1879, Chief Iron Eye and Bright Eyes set out for Fort Omaha from their reservation near Decatur, Nebraska. Since they likely had left without government permission, they could be arrested at any time. But they were desperate to get help for their cousins. They believed General Crook needed to hear the full story of the suffering and deaths the Poncas sustained in Indian Territory and the reason Standing Bear and his companions had made their arduous journey to come home in the middle of winter.[10]

Chief Iron Eye knew General Crook was a member of the Omaha Tribe's secret society, the Soldier Lodge. So he likely believed General Crook respected him enough to meet with him. He took his daughter Bright Eyes with him as interpreter, because she was fluent in English as well as the Ponca and Omaha languages.

They met with General Crook in his office at Fort Omaha on Saturday evening March 29, 1879, and told him the sad story of the Ponca's ordeal for the past two years. Crook was so disturbed by what he heard that he decided to share this information with someone he knew could help the Poncas. That person was Thomas Tibbles, a fellow member of the Soldier Lodge and the deputy editor of Omaha's largest newspaper, the *Omaha Daily Herald*. Crook knew Tibbles and likely felt he could trust him. Crook had enlisted Tibbles's aid in 1877 with Spotted Tail, chief of the Brule, regarding another government order that Crook did not support.[11]

### The Midnight Ride

Around midnight General Crook took Chief Iron Eye and Bright Eyes on the four-mile ride to meet with Tibbles at the office of the *Omaha Daily Herald* at 257 Farnam Street, Omaha.[12] They arrived at 1:00 a.m. on Sunday, March 30. For the next three and a half hours, the chief and his daughter told Tibbles the entire two-year story of what the Poncas and Standing Bear had endured. The meeting ended at 4:30 a.m. Crook told Tibbles that the fate of Standing Bear and his people was now in his hands.[13]

Tibbles confirmed that he was working late in his office that Saturday night because he had to do the work of two editors, as the editor-in-chief was out of town. He said that at around 11 p.m. an assistant informed him that a group of Poncas were being held prisoner at Fort Omaha after leaving Indian Territory without permission. That was likely all Tibbles knew about the arrest until Chief Iron Eye and Bright Eyes told him the rest of the story a few hours later.[14]

### Evidence of Chief Iron Eye and Bright Eyes at Meeting

A day later Crook interviewed Standing Bear and listened as the chief told his story of the past two years. At the end of the interview, Crook told the interpreter, "I have heard all of this story before. It is just as they say."[15] So the question arises, how had General Crook learned of the entire Ponca story, beginning with their forced removal two years earlier, and from whom?

There is no direct evidence that Chief Iron Eye and Bright Eyes were the source for General Crook's knowledge of the entire Ponca story, or even that they accompanied the general to visit Tibbles. But the circumstantial evidence is strong and credible. Chief Iron Eye and Bright Eyes were the only people who had direct contact with Standing Bear and the Poncas for the previous two years at the critical times in the story. Standing Bear trusted them completely. They were family. They had first-hand knowledge of what the government had done to the Poncas:

1. They cared for and listened to Standing Bear and the other Ponca Chiefs in March 1877 after the chiefs had walked five hundred miles to the Omaha village from Indian Territory and lived in their homes for a few days.
2. They spent three days in late May 1877 with Standing Bear and the Ponca people near Columbus, Nebraska, during the forced removal and listened to their cries.
3. They cared for Standing Bear and his companions for over two weeks in March 1879 after the Poncas' escape from Indian Territory.
4. They were present when the soldiers arrested Standing Bear and his companions.

There is one more piece of evidence to consider. At that time George Crook lived with his wife Mary at 596 Eighteenth Street in Omaha.[16] The Crooks did not move into the newly built home at Fort Omaha (today known as "the Crook House") until the fall of 1879. So General Crook would have no other reason to still be in his office at Fort Omaha at midnight on a Saturday evening except for his meeting with the chief and his daughter. The general could easily have gone home at a normal hour, had dinner with his wife as was his custom, and then met Tibbles at a reasonable time on Sunday morning. Obviously he understood that in order to ensure that Iron Eye and Bright Eyes could have an opportunity to share their story with Tibbles, he would have to take them into downtown Omaha under the cover of darkness so they could avoid being recognized and arrested, putting his professional reputation as an army commander at risk.

Bright Eyes became an important source of information for Tibbles in the days that followed. Addison E. Sheldon confirmed this fact after he visited Standing Bear in 1904, saying, "When Standing Bear of the Ponca Indians who had escaped from Oklahoma came to the Omaha Tribe for help in 1879, Bright Eyes at once became the champion of the poor Poncas. She wrote to the newspapers the story of their wrongs. She visited Omaha in their behalf. While thus engaged she became acquainted with Mr. T. H. Tibbles, an editorial writer for the Omaha Herald."[17]

### Summary

The evidence is convincing that the only credible source of General Crook's knowledge concerning the entire story of the Ponca ordeal came from Bright Eyes and Chief Iron Eye.

While Chief Iron Eye added stature to the meeting, Bright Eyes was a highly educated linguist, fluent in Ponca, Omaha, and English. Her passion for her cousins, and her evident fear the government might move her own people from their ancestral homeland to Indian Territory, must have impressed General Crook. It inspired him to seek help from Tibbles, the one person he knew would be just as passionate to fight such injustice.

It was up to Thomas Tibbles to take the next step.

Fig. 9. Thomas H. Tibbles, 1900. Deputy editor of the *Omaha Daily Herald* at the time of the trial. Courtesy History Nebraska RG2737-04.

Fig. 10. *Omaha Daily Herald* office (office of Thomas Tibbles), second floor above billiard saloon, Thirteenth and Douglas Streets, Omaha (newspaper employees leaning out of the windows). Courtesy of the Bostwick-Frohardt Collection owned by KM3TV and on permanent loan to the Durham Museum, Omaha, BF14–275.

# 10

## The Interviews

On Sunday morning, March 30, 1879, after only a few hours' sleep, Thomas Tibbles awoke knowing it was crucial for him to meet with Standing Bear. He needed to confirm the grievous story he had just heard from General Crook, Chief Iron Eye, and Bright Eyes. It took him about an hour to walk four miles to Fort Omaha to interview Standing Bear and the other prisoners.[1]

---

### Thomas H. Tibbles (1840–1928)

Thomas Henry Tibbles was born on May 24, 1840, near Athens, Ohio. He led a very colorful life before and after this story. At a young age, he left home to become an assistant to Gen. James Lane in the fight against slavery in Kansas. At that time, he met abolitionist John Brown and narrowly escaped being hanged by a proslavery mob. For a time he lived with the Omaha Tribe and learned their language. In 1856 he was initiated into the Soldier Lodge, a secret and honorary recognition by the tribe because of his common bond with them.[2] On October 1, 1861, he married an Englishwoman, Amelia Owens, in Pennsylvania. They had two daughters, Eda and May. During the Civil War he served as a scout and a reporter. After the war he was a circuit preacher for the Episcopal Church. But in order to provide better support for his family, he left that ministry and moved to Omaha in 1871, to be a reporter for an Omaha newspaper.[3] He was thirty-nine years old at the time of the trial.

---

### Tibbles Interviews Ponca Prisoners

At first Standing Bear was reluctant to speak with Tibbles. He was concerned that it was not respectful to speak to anyone before his scheduled meeting with General Crook the next day. So Tibbles showed Standing Bear a few of the secret signs of the Soldier Lodge, which Standing Bear recognized instantly. He then reached out to shake Tibbles's hand. Together the group shared the pipe of peace.[4]

The interview Tibbles conducted with Standing Bear and his fellow Ponca prisoners was reported in the April 1, 1879, morning edition of the *Omaha Daily Herald*. Charles Morgan acted as the interpreter.

Buffalo Chip (Ta-zha-but), chief of the Ponca Medicine Clan, spoke first. Tibbles said, "He spoke, talking slowly, and making emphatic gestures occasionally, as follows":

When I was young, the gun was the greatest friend the Indian had ... The gun is not my friend now. The greatest friend I have is the plow. The game (*buffalo*) is gone never to come back. I look everywhere and I see none. It has vanished away like a dream when I wake from sleep. But the ground is here. It can never vanish away. From the ground the Indian must live. . . . We talked among ourselves years ago. We agreed that we would raise cattle, horses, pigs and all kinds of stock. We said we would learn to plow, we would build houses out of wood, we would learn to do like the white people. . . . We told the men the Great Father sent to talk to us that we would do this years ago. We have kept our word. We have taught our hands to hold the plow handles. We built houses. We raised stock. Now look at us today. See these rags. We have no houses, no stock, no grain, we are prisoners in this camp, and we have never committed any crime.[5]

When Buffalo Chip stopped speaking, Tibbles waited patiently. After a brief period of silence, Buffalo Chip continued:

Eight days ago, I was at work on my farm which the Omaha's gave me. I had sowed some spring wheat and wished to sow some more. I was living peaceably with all men. I have never committed any crime. I was arrested and brought back as a prisoner. Does your law do that? I have been told since the great war that all men were free men, and that no man can be made a prisoner unless he does wrong. I have done no wrong, and yet I am here a prisoner. Have you a law for white men and a different law for those who are not white?[6]

Tibbles noticed that "a feeling of solemnity came over all; they seemed to think death was very near in any event." Tibbles was especially moved by the sight of a young woman sitting in the back of the lodge holding a baby close to herself, rocking "back and forth with tears running down over her face."[7]

Again a period of silence came over the room. Charles Morgan, an interpreter for the Omaha Tribe, turned to Tibbles and whispered, "This is awful. These men are my friends. They are of my blood."[8]

Tibbles asked Buffalo Chip what should be done "in reference to the Indians and how the government should deal with them." Buffalo Chip replied:

It seems to me that the government should let the Indians go on some land that is good, where good crops could be raised. This land should be given them for theirs forever, given so the government could not take it away, so that the white men could not get it. Indians cannot make plows and axes and wagons, so the government should give them some to help them start. And they can't plow where the ground is all hills and stones like it is down where the Ponca reservation is.[9]

At this point in the interview, Buffalo Chip suggested that a judicial system should be established to benefit both parties:

There should be laws to govern the Indians the same as the whites. A court should be established where those who do wrong, both Indians and white men, should be tried. We have never had a court. If white men steal our ponies, there is nobody to punish them. If the Indians do wrong, they make the tribe responsible and the soldiers come out and kill our people. We want land which shall be our own and we want a court. Let those who do right be protected and those who do wrong be punished.[10]

When Buffalo Chip finished, Standing Bear began to speak. He explained the horrors suffered by his people while living in Indian Territory:

The first four months we were there, Agent Howard never issued us a pound of rations. We were all nearly starved to death. . . . Starvation so reduced our strength that when the sickness came on in the fall they could not stand it, and our people began to die. It was like a great house with a big fire in it, and everything was poison. We never saw such sickness before. One hundred and fifty of our people have died and more are dying every day. . . . It is the worst country in the world. It was a place made to die in and not to live in. There is no land there which will raise anything, and we have nothing to farm with, for they never brought us the things they took away.[11]

Standing Bear also told Tibbles of his personal tragedies and the reason he decided to make the dangerous journey home in the middle of a very hard winter:

My son died, my sister died and my brother there was near dying. We had nothing to do but sit still, be sick, starve and die. My son who died was a good boy, I did everything I could to help educate him, that when I was gone, he could live like the white men and teach these little ones (pointing to some little children). I am too old to learn to read and write and speak English. . . . My boy who died down there, as he was dying looked up to me and said, I would like you to take my bones back and bury them there where I was born. I promised him I would. I could not refuse the dying words of my boy. I have attempted to keep my word. His bones are in that trunk.[12]

Near the end of the interview Susette Primo, Standing Bear's wife, motioned to Tibbles that she wished to speak. "With eyes full of tears," she said:

My mother is buried there, my grandmother and another child. My boy was a good boy and we tried to do what he wanted us to do. We were just getting ready to bury him when the soldiers came upon us. Won't you go to General Crook and ask him if we must go back south, to let us have time to take him back to the Agency and bury him? My heart is broken. My eyes are full of tears all the time, and ever since I came to this place there is an ache here (laying her hand on her heart). If we must go back, these little children will soon die too.[13]

After Standing Bear's wife spoke, Tibbles reported "such a feeling of depression and utter hopelessness settled down over all, that the Herald representative [himself] arose and left the lodge and walked around outside a few moments." When Tibbles returned, Standing Bear said, "We want to be under the same law as the white men. We want to be free."[14]

*Tibbles Races to Seek Clergy Help*

Tibbles's interview with the Ponca prisoners lasted for three hours.[15] He realized he needed a plan to inform as many influential people as possible. The Poncas' story had to be told quickly before the Poncas were taken back to Indian Territory. So he decided his first move would be to contact as many churches in Omaha as possible. He needed their help in appealing to Secretary Schurz to revoke his order of removal, so he started running.[16]

The first church Tibbles reached was the Presbyterian church, pastored by Rev. W. J. Harsha. He received permission to speak to the congregation after the sermon. Next, he went to the Congregational Church, pastored by Rev. A. F. Sherrill. He was allowed to speak between the hymns. He visited other churches and asked each pastor to sign a resolution requesting Interior Secretary Schurz to revoke the removal order. Rev. E. H. E. Jameson, pastor of a Baptist Church and an old friend of Carl Schurz, wrote the following telegram, signed by four pastors, and sent the next day.[17]

### Telegram to Secretary Carl Schurz

Omaha, Neb. March 31, 1879
To Hon. Carl Schurz, Secretary of the Interior
Washington:

Seven lodges of Ponca Indians, who had settled on Omaha reservation, and were commencing to work at farming, have, by your order, been arrested to be taken south. I beseech you as a friend to have this order revoked. Several churches and congregations have passed resolutions recommending that these Indians be permitted to remain with the Omahas. Some of the Indians are too sick to travel. Particulars by mail.

> E. H. E. Jameson, Pastor Baptist Church
> H. D. Fisher, Pastor Methodist Church
> W. J. Harsha, Pastor Presbyterian Church
> A. F. Sherrill, Pastor Congregational Church

Tibbles arrived home about 11:00 p.m. After eating a quick supper, he transcribed the notes of his interview with Standing Bear and the other Ponca prisoners. It took him six hours. After just two hours of sleep, he

returned to Fort Omaha to witness a most unusual interview with General
Crook and the Poncas, which he reported in the April 1, 1879, edition of the
*Omaha Daily Herald*.[18]

Lt. John G. Bourke, aide-de-camp to General Crook for over two decades,
recorded General Crook's interview with the prisoners in his diary. Bourke
started writing a diary during his days at West Point. He continued making
entries in his diary until his death.[19] Bourke's diary is in important source
of primary information for this period in Ponca history.

### John G. Bourke (1846–96)

John Gregory Bourke was born June 23, 1846, in Philadelphia. After grad-
uating from West Point he received the Medal of Honor for his bravery at
the battle of Stones River, Tennessee, in 1862. He was an accomplished
linguist (i.e., Latin, Greek, Gaelic, Apache) and the author of many books
and articles focused on Southwest Native American ethnology. He married
Mary Horbach of Omaha in 1883, and they had three children. He died
of a heart attack on June 8, 1896, in Philadelphia at the age of forty-nine
and is buried with his wife in Arlington National Cemetery.

### *General Crook Interviews Ponca Prisoners*

On March 31, 1879, General Crook met with Standing Bear and other Ponca
prisoners in his office at Fort Omaha. The interview began at noon and
lasted two hours. It was unusual for the commanding general of the United
States Department of the Platte, as the arresting officer, to meet with his
prisoners, considered under the law to be "wards of the government." But
General Crook treated Native Americans differently than most military
officers did at the time, and he respected their known desire to be given an
opportunity to speak for themselves. Bourke reported that eighteen people
were present at the meeting, including:

- Eight representatives of the military: Brigadier General George
  Crook, Lieut-col. Robert Williams, Ass't Adjt Genl. Lieut-col. Wm.
  B. Royall, Inspector General, Colonel M.I. Ludington, Chief Qr.
  Master, General John H. King, Col 9th Infantry, Captain A.S. Burt,
  9th Infantry, Lieut. W.L. Carpenter, 9th Infantry, and Lieut. John G.
  Bourke, 3 Cavalry, A.D.C;

- ▸ Eight members of the Ponca Tribe: Buffalo Chip, Cries for War, Yellow Horse, Long Runner, Crazy Bear, Buffalo Track, Little Duck, and Standing Bear;
- ▸ Charles Morgan, an Omaha Indian, who acted as interpreter;
- ▸ Thomas H. Tibbles of the *Omaha Herald*.[20]

Before recording the interview, Bourke wrote a brief description of Standing Bear in his diary:

> A noble-looking Indian, tall and commanding in presence, dignified in manner and very elegantly dressed in the costume of his tribe. He wore a shirt made of blue flannel, having collar and cuffs of red cloth, ornamented with brass buttons, leggings of blue flannel, moccasins of deer-skin, and over his shoulders was draped a beautiful blanket, one-half red, the other half blue, with the lines of suture covered by a broad band of beadwork. The most striking feature in his attire was a necklace of claws of the grizzly bear of which he appeared highly proud.[21]

Bourke reported that General Crook and the officers shook hands with the Poncas, who "then squatted in a semi-circle on the floor."[22] Crook motioned to Charles Morgan that the chiefs could begin speaking. Standing Bear stood up and shook hands with General Crook for a second time. He addressed him and the other officers in friendship, sharing a brief history of his people:

> We have come back from the ocean, the great water to the East . . . and we have traveled until we have got to Dacotah Territ. A good many of our tribe have lived there on that old reservation. Somebody came there to our reservation and took us to another reservation. I had built my house with my own hand, broke the land, had horses and cattle. Then somebody else came there and threw my things away.[23]

After describing the sufferings and deaths in the two years the Poncas lived in Indian Territory, Standing Bear made his plea for help:

> My brothers, it just seems this way to me; as if a big prairie-fire was coming towards me: I would take hold of my wife and baby boy and run with them to a safe place. As if the Great River was overflowing, I'd

Fig. 11. Gen. George Crook, commander of the Department of the Platte, 1879. Courtesy Douglas County Historical Society.

try to get them up on the hills, out of danger. The Almighty has looked down upon me. He knows what I am saying. I think he has given me reason to say these words. I hope the Almighty may send a good spirit to my brothers and make them think of me . . . Oh, my brothers and my friends outside! I want you to look at me and take pity on me and help me to save my women and children. I need help.[24]

General Crook responded to Standing Bear's plea saying, "I think myself it is a very hard case—but it is something I haven't anything to do with. I must obey my orders from Washington. We will give them plenty to eat while they are here. I know it's very hard and painful for them to go down and it's just as hard and painful for us to have to send them there."[25] Bourke ended his diary entry for March 31, 1879, reporting that the meeting concluded with more handshaking.[26]

George Crook was a powerful force in this story. Standing Bear and the Poncas would have been sent back to Indian Territory without a trial had it not been for General Crook. He was willing to meet with Chief Iron Eye and Bright Eyes to hear the plight of the Poncas. He then took them to the office of Thomas Tibbles on a midnight ride, so they could personally tell Tibbles the Ponca story, at risk to his own reputation. The next day Crook met the prisoners in his own office to allow them to tell their story, a clear indication of his respect for the Poncas.

### April 1, 1879, Edition of the Omaha Daily Herald

Tibbles walked back to his office at the *Omaha Daily Herald* to transcribe his notes from the meeting at General Crook's office. He arrived midafternoon and didn't finish his article until 3:30 a.m.[27] The *Omaha Daily Herald* printed an historic edition of its newspaper on April 1, 1879. His article was picked up by newspapers across the United States with favorable editorials in the *Chicago Tribune, Missouri Republican, New York Herald, New York Tribune*, and *New York Sun*. The article created a national interest in the Ponca tragedy.[28] The *Omaha Daily Herald* reported the story in a series of headlines:

## CRIMINAL CRUELTY

The History of the Ponca
Prisoners Now at the Barracks

A Tale of Cruelty
That Was Never Surpassed

Now They Have Been
Wronged and Robbed

Gen. Crook Holds a Council With Them.

The article contained detailed information of the Tibbles interview with the Ponca prisoners, transcribing the remarks of Buffalo Chip, Standing Bear, and Susette Primo, as well as a few words by Charles Morgan. Tibbles reported the extraordinary meeting held at General Crook's office with Standing Bear and other Ponca chiefs. He concluded the article by providing the readers with a copy of the Omaha clergy's Resolution to Carl Schurz.[29]

*Newspaper Identifies Prisoners*

This same edition of the *Omaha Daily Herald* listed the names of the twenty-six Ponca prisoners held at Fort Omaha:[30]

| THE EIGHT MEN | THE SIX BOYS |
| --- | --- |
| Standing Bear (Ma-chu-nah-zha) | Turtle Grease (Ka-wig-i-sha) |
| Buffalo Chip (Ta-zha-but) | Walk in the Mud (Min-i-chuck) |
| Yellow Horse (Shan-gu-he-zhe) | Walk in the Wind (Ta-do-mon-e) |
| Cries for War (Na-chen-ah-gaz) | Coon's Tail (Me-gah-sin-de) |
| Long Runner (Wa-the-ha-cuh-she) | Big Mouth (E-tun-ka) |
| Crazy Bear (Ma-chu-dun) | Swift (Wa-thi-ka) |
| Little Duck (Me-tha-zhun-ga) | |
| Buffalo Track (Ta-the-ga-da) | |

| THE TWELVE WOMEN AND GIRLS | |
| --- | --- |
| Buffalo Cow (Ta-wau-oo) | Good Provision (Oo-moo-ah) |
| Midst of the Sun (Me-he-da-wah) | Wa-gang-wah |
| Feather Crazy (Me-shud-da-de) | Little Buffalo Woman (Ta-nigh-ingah) |
| Yellow Spotted Buffalo (Za-zi-zi) | Susette Primo (Standing Bear's wife) |
| Walking Yellow (Za-on-a) | Midst of the Eagles (Me-he-da-wah) |
| Grown Hair (No-zha-zhe) | Laura Primo (Susette's niece) |

Today the name of Standing Bear is well known. However, few people know or have heard the names of his fellow prisoners, who were just as affected by the injustice, the physical and emotional sufferings, and the deaths of friends and family. Their homes, land and way of life had also been taken from them.

*Summary*

General Crook had taken Omaha Chief Iron Eye and his daughter Bright Eyes on a midnight ride to tell the entire Ponca story to newspaper editor Thomas Tibbles. For over three hours, Tibbles listened as they shared the heartbreaking story of the Poncas' forced removal to Indian Territory, their subsequent arrest, and imminent return.

Tibbles and Crook both interviewed the Ponca prisoners to hear the story first-hand from them. Tibbles then secured the support of various members of the Omaha clergy who sent a telegram to President Hayes on behalf of the Poncas. He also wrote a detailed report published by the *Omaha Daily Herald* and disseminated nationally.

Yet, in spite of the support for the Poncas in various newspaper editorials in major Eastern cities, Secretary Schurz did not rescind his order to have the Ponca prisoners taken back to Indian Territory. General Crook would be forced to escort his prisoners back to Indian Territory as soon as the sick among them were able to travel.

Time was running out.

Tibbles needed to find a lawyer.

# 11

## Tibbles Assembles a Legal Team

Tibbles faced a dilemma. A lawyer was needed to take this unprecedented case. Such a lawyer must possess the creative skill to draft unique pleadings, and the persuasive skill to argue the case before a federal judge for the first time in an American courtroom. Even if Tibbles could find such a lawyer, he would have to convince him of the historic importance of the case and the necessity of representing the prisoners for free.

Would any successful lawyer in Omaha be willing to risk his reputation and future standing in the community to represent this group of Native Americans? *Wolfe's City Directory* for 1878–79 stated that the population of Omaha was 26,215, nearly twenty-five years after its founding. There were fifty-nine active attorneys.[1] On the evening of April 2, 1879, Tibbles found his man, John L. Webster.

---

### John L. Webster (1847–1929)

John Lee Webster was born on March 18, 1847, in Harrison County, Ohio. After being wounded in the Civil War, he attended Mount Union College in Ohio and Washington College in Pennsylvania. With his wife, Josephine Watson, he settled by accident in Omaha in 1869. He was headed to Wyoming to open a law office, but due to a blizzard his train was forced to stay in Omaha for a week. During that time he decided Omaha would be a good place to live and work. He became one of the most distinguished lawyers and civic leaders in the history of Omaha, serving in the state legislature, as Omaha city attorney, and most importantly as president of the Nebraska Constitutional Convention in 1875. His law office was located at 244 Douglas Street in Omaha. At the time of the Standing Bear trial, he was thirty-two years of age.[2]

---

### Tibbles Calls on Webster

Tibbles had a connection with John Webster. Both had attended Mount Union College in Ohio. Tibbles went to Webster's home at 380 Chicago

Street in Omaha to describe the facts of the case. He considered him to be "a hard student and a man whose opinions commanded respect in the courts and outside."[3] Webster was moved, but said he needed to "take the matter under advisement."[4] Tibbles returned in the morning and Webster agreed to take the case under one condition: Tibbles must secure the services of A. J. Poppleton as co-counsel.

Referring to Poppleton, Webster told Tibbles, "I know of no lawyer in these United States who can handle these underlying, fundamental questions of government and human liberty more ably than he."[5] Tibbles felt the same, saying, Poppleton "was considered without a peer in the legal profession in the State, and that as an orator there were few in the whole country who could so entrance an audience."[6]

### Tibbles Calls on Poppleton

On April 4, 1879, Tibbles met with A. J. Poppleton in his office located in the headquarters of the Union Pacific Railroad (the former Herndon House Hotel) at the northeast corner of Ninth and Farnam Streets in downtown Omaha.[7] Poppleton listened carefully as Tibbles related the Poncas story. In his *Reminiscences*, Poppleton gave the reason he had agreed to take the case:

> I was requested to join Mr. J. L. Webster in an application for a habeas corpus to test the validity of the restraint of the liberty of Standing Bear for the purpose of removing him to Indian Territory. The question of whether the writ would lie on behalf of a tribal Indian and also whether the United States had any lawful power by its soldiery to remove him were wholly new and of vast importance. Without fee or reward or any hope or promise of compensation, Mr. Webster and myself entered upon this work and espoused the cause of the Indians.[8]

---

### Andrew J. Poppleton (1830–96)

Andrew Jackson Poppleton was born on July 24, 1830, in Oakland County, Michigan. After the law firm he worked for in Detroit dissolved, he read an article in the *New York Tribune* about a new city west of Council Bluffs. He set out to see it for himself. In his autobiography, *Reminiscences*, Poppleton wrote that while walking in downtown Omaha on October 14, 1854, he discovered that "there were perhaps twenty people on the site

Fig. 12. (*left*) Andrew J. Poppleton, attorney for Standing Bear and Ponca prisoners and Omaha's first practicing lawyer. Courtesy Bostwick-Frohardt Collection owned by KM3TV and on permanent loan to Durham Museum, Omaha, BF3217–077.

Fig. 13. (*right*) John L. Webster, attorney for Standing Bear and Ponca prisoners, president of Nebraska Constitutional Convention, 1875. Courtesy History Nebraska, RG2141–23.

of the present city of Omaha, but there was no government, no courts, no laws. For legal work, it seemed an unpromising field."[9] He decided to leave Omaha. While walking out of town, he ran into an old friend from Michigan, A. J. Hanscom, who assured him a territorial organization was being set up and asked him to consider staying. Poppleton agreed and opened the first law office in Omaha in 1854. He built a 10'x14' cottonwood and sod structure near Tenth and Farnam Streets that functioned as his home and law office. He served in the first territorial legislature in 1855, and in that same year married New York native Caroline Laura Sears in Council Bluffs, Iowa. He was twenty-five and she was twenty. Two years later he was elected speaker of the legislature. In 1858 he was elected Omaha's second mayor. Poppleton left private practice in the mid-1860s to become general counsel for the Union Pacific Railroad. Joseph Barker, one of the first settlers of Omaha, wrote "at the breaking of the ground for the Union Pacific Railroad it is said that Poppleton spoke so eloquently that he was asked to handle the Company's legal business in Nebraska."[10] At the time of the Trial of Standing Bear, he was forty-nine years of age.

*Summary*

Tibbles had done the job General Crook encouraged him to do. He had published a story for national dissemination, encouraged local community involvement, and brought together two of the most distinguished lawyers in Omaha to represent Standing Bear and the Ponca prisoners.

Time was of the essence.

Now it was up to the lawyers.

# 12

## The Great Writ

Webster and Poppleton believed the only legal solution to stop General Crook from being forced to carry out the government's Order of Removal was to get Standing Bear and the other Ponca prisoners into federal court. To accomplish this task, the lawyers decided to file an application for a writ of habeas corpus, thereby placing a hold on the government's order until a hearing could be held.

Andrew Poppleton credited General Crook with the idea of using a writ of habeas corpus in this matter, saying, "It is within my personal knowledge that General Crook was the first person to suggest the remedy of habeas corpus. I believe him to have been the first person who ever conceived the idea that the great writ would lie at the suit of a tribal Indian. This, in my judgment, is not the least of his titles to the affection and gratitude of his country."[1]

Webster did not believe that a writ of habeas corpus had ever been filed before in a federal court on behalf of Native Americans. He explained his thinking to Tibbles:

This is a question of vast importance. A Petition for such a Writ must be based upon broad constitutional grounds, and the principles involved in it underlie all personal liberty. It is a question of the natural rights of men, such as was discussed by the fathers and founders of this government. I am not satisfied that a Writ would hold on account of the peculiar relations of Indians to the government. They have always been treated as "wards," as incapable of making contracts, etc., but it will do no harm to try. It seems to me that there ought to be power somewhere to stop this inhuman cruelty, and if it does not reside in the courts where shall we find it? If the Hon. A. J. Poppleton will assist me, I will go right to work and draw up the papers.[2]

While Webster and Poppleton began to draft the application for the writ, Tibbles went to a law library in downtown Omaha to find a legal way to connect the writ directly to the Poncas since they were considered wards of the government, not persons. He had some familiarity with the law because he had worked in a law office in Winterset, Iowa, twenty-five years earlier.

### The Fourteenth Amendment

After many hours of research, Tibbles found the solution to connect the writ to the Poncas—the Fourteenth Amendment to the Constitution. The amendment had been enacted in 1866 and ratified by the states on July 28, 1868. Section 1 of the Fourteenth Amendment contained the key language:

> All persons born or naturalized in the United States, and subject to the jurisdiction thereof, are citizens of the United States and of the State wherein they reside. No state shall make or enforce any law which shall abridge the privileges or immunities of citizens of the United States; nor shall any State deprive any person of life, liberty, or property, without due process of law; nor deny to any person within its jurisdiction the equal protection of the laws.[3]

In their research the lawyers discovered a report issued on December 14, 1870, by the Senate Judiciary Committee, chaired by Senator Carpenter. The committee was directed to inquire into what effect the Fourteenth Amendment would have on Native Americans. The report stated that the amendment would apply to them only if they had separated from their tribe:

> Volumes of treaties, acts of Congress almost without number, the solemn adjudications of the highest judicial tribunal of the republic, and the universal opinion of our statesmen and people, have united to exempt the Indian, being a member of a tribe recognized by, and having treaty relations with, the United States from the operation of our laws, and the jurisdiction of our courts. Whenever we have dealt with them, it has been in their collective capacity as a state, and not with their individual members *except when such members were separated from the tribe* to which they belonged; and then we have asserted such jurisdiction as every nation exercises over the subjects of another independent sovereign nation entering its territory and violating its laws (emphasis added).[4]

Webster and Poppleton now believed they had persuasive grounds to connect the Ponca prisoners to the writ, because they had separated from their tribe.

### Definition

Habeas corpus is a Latin term that means "present the body." A writ of habeas corpus is an order issued by a judge commanding the person detaining a prisoner to present that prisoner before the court, in order to test the legality of the imprisonment.[5]

It is called "the Great Writ" because it is the guardian of all other rights against the lawless action of the government. The United States Supreme Court stated that "although in form the Great Writ is simply a mode of procedure, its history is inextricably intertwined with the growth of fundamental rights of personal liberty. For its function has been to provide a prompt and efficacious remedy for whatever society deems to be intolerable restraints."[6]

### The Magna Carta of 1215

The first written expression of the writ of habeas corpus occurred on June 15, 1215, when John, king of England, was forced to sign the Magna Carta at Runnymede. Today, eight hundred years later, the Magna Carta is considered one of the bulwarks of our freedom. Within its sixty-three clauses are two which speak to the purpose of the writ:

> Clause 39. No free man shall be taken or imprisoned or disseized or outlawed or exiled or in any way ruined, nor will we go or send against him, except by the lawful judgment of his peers, or by the law of the land. Clause 40. To no one will we sell, to no one will we deny or delay right or justice.[7]

### Habeas Corpus Act of 1679

The British Parliament formally adopted the Habeas Corpus Act in 1679, setting forth the process by which the writ could be employed by a person accused of criminal behavior:

> That on complaint and request in writing, by or on behalf of any person committed and charged with any crime (except for treason or felony, expressed in the warrant, or as accessory, or on suspicion thereof),

the Chancellor or a Judge shall award a Habeas Corpus for such prisoner, returnable immediately before himself or any other of the judges,
and upon giving security to appear and answer to the accusation in the
proper court of judicature. . . . That the Writ shall be returned, and the
prisoner brought up, within a limited time, according to the distances,
not exceeding twenty days.[8]

In his landmark *Commentaries on the Laws of England* (1750), Sir William
Blackstone, justice in His Majesty's Court of Common Pleas, explained that
the 1679 act removed the injury caused by illegal confinement of a prisoner
because "it frequently happens that parties suffer a long imprisonment
because they are forgotten."[9]

### The Writ in American Law

Article I, Section 9 of the Constitution of the United States declared that
"the privilege of the writ of habeas corpus shall not be suspended, unless
when in cases of rebellion or invasion the public safety may require it."[10]

The First Congress enacted the Judiciary Act of 1789, by which federal
courts were granted power to hear applications for a writ of habeas corpus
filed on behalf of persons jailed under federal authority.[11]

Then came the Civil War. On April 27, 1861, President Abraham Lincoln
told Winfield Scott, commanding general of the United States Army, that if
there was armed resistance in Maryland against the federal troops traveling
through the state on their way to defend Washington DC in the first month
of the Civil War, Scott or his officers in command were authorized to suspend habeas corpus in order to guarantee the safety of the troops. Armed
resistance came and bridges were destroyed. Members of the Maryland
state militia were arrested, including John Merryman, who was charged
with treason against the federal government and taken to Fort McHenry for
detainment. His lawyers filed an action in federal court and Chief Justice
Roger B. Taney ruled that only Congress, not the president, had authority
under the Constitution to suspend habeas corpus.[12]

Congress passed the Habeas Corpus Suspension Act of 1863 authorizing the
president to suspend habeas corpus during the remainder of the Civil War.[13]

After the Civil War ended, Congress enacted the Habeas Corpus Act of
1867. This act expanded the application of the writ under the Judiciary Act
of 1789 from "persons jailed under federal authority," to henceforward

authorize all courts, state and federal, to hear applications for "any person restrained in violation of the Constitution, or of any treaty or law of the United States."[14]

### The Poncas' Application for a Writ (April 4, 1879)

Webster and Poppleton drafted the following Application for a Writ of Habeas Corpus on behalf of the thirty Ponca prisoners:

IN THE DISTRICT COURT OF THE
UNITED STATES,
FOR THE DISTRICT OF NEBRASKA.
THE UNITED STATES EX REL.
MA-CHU-NAH-ZHA (STANDING BEAR)
VS.
GEORGE CROOK, A BRIGADIER GENERAL
OF THE ARMY OF THE UNITED STATES,
AND COMMANDER OF THE DEPARTMENT
OF THE PLATTE.

In the matter of the Application of Má-Chu-Nah-Zha, Standing Bear et al. for a Writ of Habeas Corpus.

To the Honorable Elmer S. Dundy, Judge of the District Court of The United States for the District of Nebraska.[15]

The Application for a Writ of Habeas Corpus listed each of the names of the Ponca prisoners, and described the purpose of the Application:

That each, and all of them are prisoners unlawfully imprisoned, detained, confined and in custody, and are restrained of their liberty under and by color of the alleged authority of the United States by George Crook, a Brigadier General of the Army of the United States, and commanding the Department of the Platte, and are so imprisoned, detained, confined and in custody, and restrained of their liberty by said George Crook at Fort Omaha on a military reservation, under the sole and exclusive jurisdiction of the United States, and located within the territory of the District of Nebraska.[16]

After a brief description of the order under which General Crook held the Poncas in custody, the attorneys stated the focal point of their argument: these Poncas had separated from their tribe:

> These complainants further represent that they are Indians, and of the nationality of the Ponca Tribe of Indians, but that for a considerable time before, and at the time of their arrest and imprisonment, as is herein more fully set forth, they were separated from the Ponca Tribe of Indians, and had been and were separated from their tribal relations to said Ponca Tribe of Indians and that so many of said Ponca Tribe of Indians as maintain their tribal relations are located in the Indian Territory.[17]

Poppleton and Webster described the Poncas at the time of their arrest and imprisonment as peaceful and working hard to support themselves:

> That your complainants at the time of their arrest and imprisonment were lawfully and peaceably residing on the Omaha reservation . . . by the consent of said Omaha Tribe of Indians . . . some of them were actually engaged in agriculture, and others were making preparations for immediate agricultural labors and were supporting themselves by their own labor, and no one of these complainants was receiving or asking support of the government of the United States. That your complainants were not violating and are not guilty of any violation of any law of the United States, civil or military, or of any treaty of the United States, for which said arrest and imprisonment were made.[18]

The two lawyers concluded their Application for the Writ with a plea requesting the court to find the continued detention of these Poncas illegal, and to order their freedom restored:

> Wherefore, these complainants say that their said imprisonment and detention is wholly illegal, and they demand that a Writ of Habeas Corpus be granted directed to the said George H. Crook, a Brigadier General of the Army of the United States commanding the Department of the Platte commanding him to have the bodies of Ma-chu-nah-zha (Standing Bear) . . . [Note: The names of the other prisoners are listed as well] . . . before your honor at a time and place therein to be specified, to do and

receive what shall, then and there be considered by your honor concerning them, together with the time and cause of their detention, and said Writ, and that the complainants may then be restored to liberty.[19]

Standing Bear and seven other Poncas signed the Application for the Writ. Poppleton and Webster signed as Attorneys for Petitioners. T. H. Tibbles and Lt. W. L. Carpenter signed as witnesses. All re-signed under oath before Homer Stull, a notary public, on April 4, 1879.[20]

### Where Is the Judge?

The attorneys were now ready to file their application in federal court and make their argument before the judge. However, Judge Dundy was out of town on a bear-hunting trip. Tibbles reported that the judge's staff did not know where he was or when he would return.[21] Two days later, on Sunday evening, April 6, 1879, the judge returned home and sent a telegram notifying the attorneys that he would hear their application in his courtroom in Lincoln, Nebraska, in two days.[22]

---

**Elmer S. Dundy (1830–96)**

Elmer Scipio Dundy was born on March 5, 1830, in Trumbull County, Ohio. While employed as a teacher and principal of a school in Pennsylvania, he decided to study law. He began his practice in 1853, in the county of Clearfield, Pennsylvania. Four years later he moved to Falls City, Nebraska, to practice law, and was shortly elected to a four-year term in the Nebraska Territorial Legislature. In 1861 he married Mary H. Robertson in Omaha. After Nebraska became a state in 1867, President Andrew Johnson nominated him to be the first judge of the United States District Court for the District of Nebraska. The Senate confirmed his appointment on April 9, 1868. He held that position for twenty-eight years until his death in 1896. At the time of the Standing Bear trial, he was forty-nine years of age.

---

### Hearing on Ponca Application for Writ (April 8, 1879)

On April 8, 1879, Webster and Poppleton boarded the train in Omaha and traveled to Lincoln to appear before Judge Dundy in the federal district courtroom located in the State Capitol building. Watson B. Smith, clerk of the federal court, endorsed the Application for the Writ and handed it to the judge. The two lawyers then made their argument in support of the application. When they were finished, Judge Dundy issued his ruling:

> It being made to appear to the Court that the said Petitioners are detained without any legal authority. It is therefore ordered, that a Writ of Habeas Corpus be allowed to issue on behalf of the said Petitioners directed to George Crook, a Brigadier General of the United States, commanding the Department of the Platte, returnable within ten days from the date of the service of said Writ upon him.[23]

Later that same day, General Crook was served the writ by Ellis L. Bierbower, deputy United States marshal. Crook was now blocked from carrying out the order issued by Interior Secretary Schurz to return the Poncas to Indian Territory. Nothing more could be done until a formal hearing could be convened in federal court. General Crook signed the Return of Service on April 11, 1879, to confirm his receipt of the writ, and it was recorded with the court file on April 18, 1879.

### The Government's Response to Judge Dundy's Order

On April 9, 1879, Secretary Carl Schurz, informed that Judge Dundy had granted the Application for the Writ in favor of the Ponca prisoners, ordered the United States Attorney General to direct Genio M. Lambertson, district attorney for the Federal District Court of Nebraska, to begin an investigation into the matter.[24]

The period between the issuing of the writ by Judge Dundy on April 8, 1879, and the opening of the trial on May 1, 1879, was a time in which the government went public in its attempt to set forth its position that it had acted within its rightful authority to remove the Ponca Tribe to Indian Territory. The government believed this small band of Poncas had left Indian Territory without government permission and should be ordered back.

On April 10, 1879, E. A. Hayt, Indian commissioner to the Poncas, wrote a letter to Secretary Schurz saying he believed the land selected in Indian Territory for the Poncas was much better for them than their homeland in the Nebraska/Dakota region. He also told Schurz that he had released to the press a summary of the government's position casting negative comments as to Standing Bear's character at the time of the move to Indian Territory.[25]

Sometime after the trial, Tibbles reported a conversation he had with Standing Bear in which he showed him Hayt's letter to Schurz that disparaged his character. Tibble reported that Standing Bear "went to his trunk and took out a large roll of papers."[26] He showed Tibbles a letter Hayt had written on government stationary dated December 18, 1877, a few months after the tribe arrived in Indian Territory, in which Hayt made the following positive statement concerning Standing Bear's character:

> This is to certify that Standing Bear is a Chief of the Ponca Indians. This tribe is at peace with the United States, and Standing Bear is recognized as a chief of said tribe, whose influence has been to preserve peace and harmony between the Ponca Indians and the United States, and as such is entitled to the confidence of all persons whom he may meet.[27]

Standing Bear then told Tibbles, "The Commissioner did not give me a good character. I got my character by a long life devoted to the advancement of my tribe."[28]

### Omaha Tribe Makes Final Appeal

Members of the Omaha Tribe signed a petition on April 21, 1879, making a public plea for the release of their cousins:

> We, the Undersigned, Omaha Indians wish publicly to declare that in consideration of the relationship existing between our tribe and those Poncas . . . we are anxious for their return to our reservation, and are willing to share with them our lands and to assist them until they can, by their industry, support themselves. They are our brothers and our sisters, our uncles and our cousins, and are willing to share what we possess with them if they can only be allowed to return and labor, improve and provide for themselves where they may live in peace, enjoy good health, and the opportunity of educating their children.[29]

Tibbles reported that the *New York Herald* wrote a story about the Omaha Tribe's appeal, saying, "The appeal of the Omaha Indians in favor of their kindred, the Ponca, is one of the most extraordinary statements ever published in America."[30]

Fig. 14. Genio M. Lambertson in his law office, 1900. Photo courtesy Charles E. Wright.

### Lambertson Briefs General Crook

United States district attorney Genio M. Lambertson, left his office in Lincoln, Nebraska, sometime during the last week of April 1879, and rode the train to Omaha to interview General Crook. They met in the general's office. Lambertson reviewed the facts of the case and discussed his strategy for the hearing. He knew nothing of Crook's involvement behind the scenes with Tibbles, Chief Iron Eye, and Bright Eyes. This would be Lambertson's first trial as U.S. district attorney since assuming his job five months earlier.[31] At the time of the Standing Bear trial he was twenty-eight years of age.

---

**Genio M. Lambertson (1850–1902)**

Genio Madison Lambertson was born on May 19, 1850, in Franklin, Indiana. He graduated from the University of Chicago in 1872, and came to Lincoln, Nebraska, two years later to practice law. In December 1878 he was appointed U.S. district attorney for Nebraska, serving in that post until 1887. He was active in the Lancaster County Bar Association. Later he served as an assistant secretary of the treasury under President Benjamin Harrison; then as an attorney to the Interstate Commerce

Commission. He died in Chicago on June 15, 1902, survived by his wife, Mary Sherwood Lambertson, and his children. He is buried in Wyuka Cemetery in Lincoln, Nebraska

---

## Summary

Two of the most prominent lawyers in Nebraska, John Webster and Andrew Poppleton, filed an application for a writ of habeas corpus on behalf of their clients, Standing Bear and his twenty-nine fellow Poncas. They argued that the writ should be granted based on an 1870 Senate Judiciary Committee report saying the Fourteenth Amendment to the Constitution would apply to Native Americans if they could show they had separated from their tribe.

On April 8, 1879, federal judge Elmer Dundy heard Webster and Poppleton's argument. He ruled in favor of their application and directed the writ be served on General Crook. The enforcement of the government's Order of Removal was now halted until a trial could be held.

The time had arrived for the historic and unprecedented trial of Standing Bear and the twenty-nine Ponca prisoners.

# 13

## Witnesses Testify

**UNITED STATES ex rel. STANDING BEAR V. CROOK**

(5 Dill.453, 25 F. Cas.695)

Circuit Court D. Nebraska. 1879.


This was a hearing upon return to writ of habeas corpus
issued against George Crook, a brigadier general of the army
of the United States at the relation of Standing Bear and other
Indians, formerly belonging to the Ponca Tribe of Indians.


A. J. Poppleton and John L. Webster, for relators.

G.M. Lambertson, U.S. Atty.

Dundy, District Judge.

*Date and Place: May 1, 1879, Omaha, Nebraska*

The trial began on Thursday morning, May 1, 1879, in the federal courthouse
in Omaha, Nebraska. It concluded late in the evening of May 2, 1879. The
start date of May 1 was confirmed by Lt. John Bourke, who sat next to General Crook at the trial,[1] and by Thomas Tibbles who reported in the May 2,
1879, edition of the *Omaha Herald*, "The Ponca Indian habeas corpus case
was begun yesterday morning."[2]

*Note*. The term "Relator" was used in the trial proceedings to identify the
person (Standing Bear and the other Ponca prisoners) upon whose complaint
or at whose instance the Writ of Habeas Corpus was issued.

The federal court was located at Fifteenth and Dodge in a three-story
building known as the U.S. Customs House.[3] The U.S. post office was located
on the first floor. The Railway Mail Service and the federal court administrative offices occupied the second floor. The U.S. customs office shared

Fig. 15. Office of the Federal Court, Omaha, Nebraska, 1879. Courtesy Bostwick-Frohardt Collection owned by KM3TV and on permanent loan to the Durham Museum, Omaha, BF828-003-5.

the third floor with the federal courtroom and jury room. No federal court had ever witnessed what was about to take place in that third-floor room.

### Omaha, Nebraska

For a city of slightly over twenty-six thousand residents, Omaha was a bustling and diverse community. It boasted three banks, four concert halls, four colleges, twelve schools, thirty-two hotels, thirty-six physicians, four railroads, two hospitals, four bowling alleys, twenty-seven billiard halls, eighteen barbers, one cooper, three gunsmiths, five livery stables, four ice dealers, two steamboat agents, three undertakers, four breweries, thirteen fire stations, and seven dentists (including the author's great-uncle John Dwyer located at 695 Sixteenth Street), three telegraph companies, one streetcar railway, and four singing societies. There were twenty-six Christian church denominations: three Baptist, four Catholic, two Congregational, three Episcopal, five Lutheran, six Methodist, two Presbyterian, and one Unitarian; plus one Jewish synagogue.[4]

### Attendees

Men and women of all ranks of society in Omaha, including members of the clergy, local lawyers, and newspaper reporters, were in attendance in the courtroom to witness the trial. Omaha had four daily newspapers at the time of the trial: *Omaha Daily Herald*, *Omaha Bee*, *Omaha Republican*, and *Omaha Evening News*.[5] These local newspapers were crucial to bringing this historic civil rights case to the attention of the national press, and hence to the general public.[6]

Of all the newspapers in Omaha at the time of the trial, the *Omaha Daily Herald* had gained a national reputation among newspapers on the East Coast, due in large part to the aggressive approach taken by its founder, George L. Miller, to promote Omaha as "the future chief city of the Missouri Valley."[7] Miller had founded the newspaper in 1865 when he was just thirty-five. He came from New York to Omaha in 1854, the same year as Andrew Poppleton. By the time he opened the newspaper's doors he had worked at a variety of occupations, including "doctor, territorial politician, real estate speculator, businessman, and post sutler at Fort Kearney."[8]

The major reporter of the trial was Thomas H. Tibbles, deputy editor of the *Omaha Daily Herald*. He was the only newspaper reporter who had personally interviewed Standing Bear and the Ponca prisoners prior to the trial. Tibbles sat directly behind the relators' table, where he observed and recorded all that occurred over the next two days.

Gen. George Crook, in full dress uniform, sat at the table alongside his legal counsel, District Attorney Genio M. Lambertson. Sitting behind the general was his aide-de-camp, Lt. John G. Bourke, and Col. Horace B. Burnham, judge advocate for the Military Department of the Platte.[9]

Standing Bear walked into the courtroom in his full chief regalia, the attire he always wore when he would have an opportunity to speak for his people.[10] He was escorted by Lt. William L. Carpenter and took his place near his legal counsel, John L. Webster and Andrew J. Poppleton. With Standing Bear was his wife Susette Primo and a grandson, the child of his deceased daughter Prairie Flower. His brother Yellow Horse was present in the courtroom, as was Buffalo Chip, chief of the Medicine Clan.[11]

The court provided Standing Bear with an interpreter because he understood very little English. However, the interpreter, William Hamilton, was there only to interact between the judge, attorneys, and Standing Bear when questions were posed to him. There is no evidence that Hamilton said anything else to Standing Bear during the trial.

Standing Bear and the other members of his tribe with him understood almost nothing of what was going on in the courtroom. The presence of Native Americans in a federal courtroom was new—there was no precedent. Standing Bear probably felt uncomfortable knowing his fate and that of his family and friends was in the hands of strangers.

Also present was Bright Eyes, Standing Bear's cousin of the Omaha Tribe, who spoke both English and the Ponca languages fluently and would serve as a trusted interpreter for him if he would be granted the opportunity to speak on his own behalf. Her father, Iron Eye, chief of the Omaha Tribe, was with her.

### Court Convened

At 10:00 a.m. Judge Elmer S. Dundy entered the courtroom and gaveled the court into session. Attorneys for both sides identified themselves and their clients. Judge Dundy presented a statement of the facts of the case before the court and directed the lawyers to proceed.

### Procedural Matters Discussed

At first "the lawyers were somewhat puzzled as to the mode of procedure to be followed in the case; various questions were discussed. There was some talk between the attorneys and court about the pleadings, and what the issue in the case really was."[12]

Poppleton said it was "the duty of the United States to establish the jurisdiction of the military to hold the Indians; and the hearing should proceed upon the sufficiency of the Return of the Writ, whether it shows valid ground for the deprivation of the liberty of the Indians." Lambertson replied that Poppleton should have filed a demurrer, or made a motion to quash/dismiss, for "unless something of that kind was done, he didn't see how an issue could be raised" regarding the validity of the arrest and imprisonment of the Poncas.[13]

Lambertson expressed his frustration that he had received a letter from the United States Department of the Interior concerning the issue of whether the Poncas had dissolved their tribal relations, but he could not offer it into evidence because it had not been sworn.[14]

The letter Lambertson referred to was written by E. J. Brooks, acting commissioner for the Department of the Interior and dated April 22, 1879. The letter began with Brooks saying to Lambertson: "I am in receipt of your communication of the 14th instant, in relation to the Application by certain Ponca Indians for a Writ of Habeas Corpus, and in which you ask for a statement of the various treaties made with the Ponca Indians; the causes which led to their removal to the Indian Territory; the reason for their deserting their reservation, etc."[15]

In his letter, Commissioner Brooks provided some details of the various treaties signed by the Poncas, and then acknowledged that the 1868 Fort Laramie Treaty took land from the Poncas and gave it to the Sioux "without the consent of the latter Indians." Brooks then gave his justification for the Ponca removal, saying: "As the Poncas and Sioux had been bitter enemies for many years, it became necessary to remove the Poncas from their reservation to save them from the destruction that would be likely to overtake them from the location of the Sioux on the Missouri River."[16]

The final part of Brooks's letter to Lambertson demonstrated his callous assessment of the condition of the Ponca tribe in Indian Territory: "During the first few months of their residence in the Indian Territory, they lost a large number by death, which is inevitable in all cases of removal of Northern Indians to a Southern latitude."[17]

In spite of not having this letter available to offer into evidence, Lambertson informed the court "he was willing to proceed and consider the question of whether they had dissolved their tribal relations."[18]

The attorneys discussed other procedural matters and then the judge directed Webster to call his first witness.[19]

### Relators' First Witness—William W. Hamilton

Webster called William W. Hamilton to the stand. After being sworn under oath, Hamilton testified he had worked as a clerk in the agency store on the

Omaha reservation for six years, having lived among the Omaha Tribe for over twelve years. He spoke both the Omaha and Ponca languages. He stated that his father had been a missionary to Native American tribes, including the Omahas, for over thirty years.[20]

Webster asked Hamilton to identify the wife and grandson of Standing Bear in the courtroom and to describe the condition of Standing Bear's family when they arrived at the village of the Omaha tribe on March 4, 1877. Hamilton saw them there at that time.[21]

Webster's strategy in calling Hamilton to the stand was to elicit testimony that would prove to the court that these Ponca prisoners intended to forever sever their tribal relations when they left Indian Territory. He would do so in three lines of questions posed to this witness.

The first line of questioning concerned the clothing worn by the Poncas when they arrived at the Omaha Tribe village. Webster wanted to show that the Poncas did not dress in the typical clothes expected of Native Americans living in a tribal environment, but they dressed as any white persons would dress:

**Webster:**       How were they supplied as to clothing?

**Hamilton:**      They had blankets, some of them, and some had coats; those that had coats wore pants and were dressed in citizen's clothes.[22]

Next, Webster wanted to prove that the prisoners were not a group from a tribe with no personal identity, but lived in separate family units, married with children, the same as any white family:

**Webster:**       You may state whether or not they were divided into families at the time when they came—whether they were married and composed families as man and wife?

**Hamilton:**      They were.

**Webster:**       And the children were children of these families?

**Hamilton:**      Yes sir, some of them were orphans, living with their relations.

**Webster:**       Which ones do you speak of as being orphans?

**Hamilton:**      There were two orphans came with them. There is one (indicating a young Indian boy who was present with the Relators in the courtroom) sitting in the woman's lap. The other is at camp.

**Webster:** Who is this woman who sits there?

**Hamilton:** She is the wife of Standing Bear, Susette.[23]

Webster's third line of questioning to this witness showed the court that the intent of the Ponca prisoners was to be self-supporting farmers, not dependent upon the government:

**Webster:** State what these Indians were engaged in after they arrived at the Omaha Agency?

**Hamilton:** What little time they stayed there they were engaged in helping the Omahas put in their crops.

**Webster:** State what ones, if any, of the Indians, the Poncas, were putting in crops for themselves?

**Hamilton:** Buffalo Chip was helping put in a crop for himself. His friends at the Omaha Agency gave him land enough to sow his wheat.

**Webster:** At the time of the arrest, state, if you know, about the amount of wheat Buffalo Chip had put in on this land which was set apart for him?

**Hamilton:** I think there must have been four or five acres sowed.[24]

Continuing in this line of questioning, Webster sought to elicit confirmation from Hamilton that all of the Poncas who were healthy were working:

**Webster:** State how many of these Poncas during their stay at the Omaha Agency, were engaged in labor—whether all were so engaged?

**Hamilton:** All that were able to, were.

**Webster:** Those who were not employed in actual labor, state why they were not?

**Lambertson:** Objection. Immaterial.

**Judge:** Overruled.

**Webster:** You may answer.

**Hamilton:** Because they were sick and unable to work.[25]

Lambertson rose to cross-examine Hamilton in an attempt to get him to describe Standing Bear as a chief of the Ponca tribe, and to acknowledge that the Poncas had brought government property with them from Indian Territory, including wagons, clothes and tents, and had received supplies from the agency store which employed this witness. Lambertson was successful in getting Hamilton to agree that not all of the Poncas went to farming ground given to them by the Omaha tribe. He wanted to demonstrate to the court that Webster's contention was incorrect.[26]

Lambertson asked Hamilton a series of questions to show the court that the prisoners were not self-supporting individuals as Webster had contended, but instead were dependent on aid from the government to provide them with shelter and transportation:

**Lambertson:**  What did they live in—tents?
**Hamilton:**  Yes sir, they brought their tents, I think.
**Lambertson:**  These tents were provided by the government?
**Hamilton:**  These tents were made by themselves.
**Lambertson:**  These wagons were furnished by the government.
**Hamilton:**  Yes sir; they brought their wagons with them.[27]

Lambertson continued this line of questioning to Hamilton concerning the type of clothing the Poncas were wearing.

**Lambertson:**  Did they have any citizens' clothes?
**Hamilton:**  Yes sir; some were, and some were not.
**Lambertson:**  Some of them wore blankets?
**Hamilton:**  Some wore blankets, pants and vests, and some wore Indian clothes throughout.
**Lambertson:**  These blankets were supplied by the government?
**Hamilton:**  Some of them—yes sir.[28]

In Webster's re-direct examination, followed by Lambertson's re-cross examination, both sides questioned Hamilton as to whether the Poncas were under the control of the Omaha tribe while living on their reservation; in effect, exchanging life on one reservation for another.

**Lambertson:**  Is there any head man in the Omaha Tribe?

| Hamilton: | No sir, not now. There was some time ago, last summer, but they put away all their chiefs and head men. |
| Webster: | They live like white men, then? |
| Hamilton: | They try to.[29] |

Hamilton left the witness stand and returned to his seat near Standing Bear.

### Relators' Second Witness—Lieutenant Carpenter

Webster then called his second witness, Lt. William L. Carpenter. After being sworn on oath, Webster asked Lt. Carpenter to confirm that he had been the arresting officer of the Poncas in late March 1879, and to describe the Poncas' physical condition when he transported them to Fort Omaha. Carpenter replied that the Poncas were "dressed in citizen's clothes" and some "were willing to work; they had been sick for some time."[30]

On cross-examination, District Attorney Lambertson asked Carpenter what appeared to be a simple question, but one that resulted in the following exchange between the two lawyers and Judge Dundy:

| Lambertson: | How many chiefs are there? |
| Webster: | Objection, question is improper cross-examination. |
| Judge: | Sustained. |
| Lambertson: | State the names of the parties arrested. |
| Webster: | Objection, question is immaterial, and the returns show that. |
| Judge: | Why is that material? |
| Lambertson: | To show these Indians have their chiefs, to whom they profess allegiance. |
| Judge: | You will have to make the witness your own to do that.[31] |

Court adjourned for lunch.

### Relators' Third Witness—Standing Bear

Court reconvened at 2:00 p.m.[32] Judge Dundy directed Webster to call his next witness. Webster called Standing Bear to the stand. Standing Bear and his court-appointed interpreter, William H. Hamilton, were sworn under oath. District Attorney Lambertson immediately objected to Standing Bear being called as a witness.[33]

Lambertson was doing his duty as prosecuting attorney to seize this issue at the first opportunity. He correctly reasoned that the United States Supreme Court had already determined that Native Americans were "wards of the Government," not persons or citizens; therefore, Standing Bear had no right or standing to testify in an American courtroom.[34]

Judge Dundy overruled his objection saying, "Anybody can be sworn. This court recognizes no distinction on account of race, color, or previous condition."[35] The judge had already committed himself to give Standing Bear and the other relators their day in court when he granted their Application for a Writ of Habeas Corpus on April 8, 1879, so he likely wasn't ready to stop the proceedings this early in the trial.

*Note*: A *witness* is "one who, being present, personally sees or perceives a thing; a beholder, spectator, or eyewitness. One who testifies to what he has seen, heard, or otherwise observed."[36]

Webster's questions to Standing Bear, through his interpreter William Hamilton, were brief. The witness's answers were equally brief. The dialogue between attorney and witness focused on what Standing Bear's family life was like when living in the Dakota/Nebraska region, in contrast to what life was like for him and the Poncas in Indian Territory.[37]

Then Webster asked Standing Bear to tell the story of how he and his people lived in Indian Territory. Lambertson objected to this question, saying the hearing was "solely as to whether these Poncas have dissolved their tribal relations." But before the judge could rule on his objection, Lambertson withdrew it. Webster told the interpreter to proceed with his question. Standing Bear's reply was interpreted by William H. Hamilton:

When we got down there, we saw that the land was not good; kick off the soil and you found stones and it was not fit to farm. They promised us money and clothing, but we have seen very little of it yet. We could not do anything; we had no strength in our bodies at all, and we kept getting weaker every day. The tribe was dying off. 158 died, I think. God wants me to live. What have I done that I am brought here! I do not know. It seems as though I have no place on earth. I want a place where I can work and support my family, and when done with life, die peaceably.[38]

At this point, Standing Bear raised his voice while testifying to such a volume that Judge Dundy instructed him "not to get excited, but to take things coolly."[39] Webster began another series of brief questions to which Standing Bear replied with equally brief answers:

| | |
|---|---|
| **Webster:** | How many were in the tribe when you left the Territory? |
| **S. Bear:** | About 581. |
| **Webster:** | How many came away with you when you came up? |
| **S. Bear:** | Thirty. |
| **Webster:** | Why did you come up to the Omaha agency? |
| **S. Bear:** | I thought I might save my wife and one child I have left. |
| **Webster:** | How many of your own children died in Indian Territory? |
| **S. Bear:** | Two died down there. My son could talk English; could read and write and was a great help to me. When I think of it, it makes me feel very bad.[40] |

Then, Webster posed a question to Standing Bear in an attempt to establish that Standing Bear's intent in leaving Indian Territory was to live the remainder of his life in his homeland and not return to the Ponca tribe in Indian Territory. Webster wanted to prove an intent to disassociate themselves from their tribe. Hamilton replied to Webster's question that Standing Bear "says when he left, they asked if he was ever coming back, and he told them if he ever came back it would not be to stay; that he wanted to go to a place where they could all work and earn their own living."[41] Finally, Webster asked Standing Bear about his role as a chief:

| | |
|---|---|
| **Webster:** | After you left the tribe in Indian Territory did you exercise your authority as a chief over those who came with you? |
| **S. Bear:** | I didn't consider myself a chief. I looked upon myself as on a level with the rest.[42] |

In his cross-examination of Standing Bear, Lambertson asked him the number of people in his band of which he was chief ("about fifty"); how many of that band had followed him up north ("about thirty"); and had he taken any government-supplied wagons and mowing machines during his journey north ("two of the wagons they have were given to them on their former reservation, and the other is one he bought himself").[43] Lambertson concluded his cross-examination of Standing Bear with two key questions:

| | |
|---|---|
| **Lambertson:** | Were you chief or head man over these Indians in Indian Territory? |
| **S. Bear:** | I don't count myself as a chief. |
| **Lambertson:** | When you left did you inform the agent that you were going to take care of yourself? |
| **S. Bear:** | I told the agent I wanted to go back. We would all die there and that I was going away to save the lives of my family and make a living. I wanted to go on to my own land, land that I had never sold. There is where I wanted to go. My son asked me when he was dying to take him back and bury him there, and I have his bones in a box with me now. I want to live there the rest of my life and to be buried there.[44] |

Webster informed the judge he had no more witnesses to call.

### Lambertson Calls No Witnesses

Judge Dundy directed Lambertson to call his first witness. But Lambertson did not call anyone.[45] Before the trial began, Lambertson may have believed since the law considered an Indian to be a "ward of the government" and not a "person," the judge would grant a motion to dismiss the case and quash the writ for lack of standing. He possibly believed there was no need to prepare any person to testify on behalf of the government. So, when he objected to Webster calling Standing Bear to testify and was quickly overruled by Judge Dundy, he likely realized his mistake. On the other hand, who could he have called as a witness? Calling General Crook to testify might have backfired due to Crook's known respect for Native Americans.

### Closing Arguments Postponed

Judge Dundy turned to Webster and Poppleton and instructed them to begin their closing argument. They had expected Lambertson to call his own witnesses, so they were not fully prepared to make their closing arguments that late in the day. In addition, they would have wanted to review the testimony presented by their own witnesses.

But Judge Dundy insisted they continue. Webster stood up and started to speak, but something dramatic happened as reported in the *Omaha Daily Herald*: "There were many ladies, citizens and army officers present and the atmosphere was stifling. Mr. Webster had uttered but a few sentences when he informed the judge that it was impossible for him to proceed, and sat down, apparently very ill."[46]

Court adjourned until ten o'clock the next morning.[47]

### *Postscript—Standing Bear Speaks with Tibbles*

Tibbles followed Standing Bear and the other prisoners back to Fort Omaha. He wanted to talk with him about the day's proceedings. Standing Bear, who had not understood most of the words spoken at the trial, was frustrated with the happenings in the courtroom. He was anxious to speak for himself and asked Tibbles to relate his desire to the judge. Tibbles returned to his office to write a summary of the events of the trial's first day for the *Omaha Daily Herald*.

# 14

## The Trial's Closing Arguments

Before the court convened for the second day of the trial, Thomas Tibbles met in private with Judge Dundy and shared Standing Bear's request to speak to the court. Judge Dundy consented.[1]

The line of questioning during the first day of the trial had focused on whether Standing Bear and the other Ponca prisoners had severed their ties to the Ponca tribe, with the intent to live on their own, as individuals, outside of Indian Territory.

As the lawyers prepared their closing arguments, they did so with full knowledge that they needed to convince only one man—Elmer S. Dundy. The judge alone would decide the outcome. This was a bench trial; there was no jury.

### A Case of "Firsts"

This was a case of "firsts." For the first time in the history of American jurisprudence, a lawyer stood in a federal courtroom representing a client who was a Native American. A client who was not a person in the eyes of the law. A client who was not a citizen in the eyes of the law. It had never been done before. This was a case of "first impression," meaning it had no precedent for lawyers or for judges.

The May 2, 1879, edition of the *New York Times* included a lead article captioned "Have Indians Any Rights. Testing the Government's Power to Remove Them." In the article the *Times* reported that the Standing Bear trial was "the first case of the kind ever brought before a United States court."[2]

### Challenges Facing the Lawyers

Webster and Poppleton were faced with an unprecedented challenge. They must be creative as well as factual in their closing arguments to persuade Judge Dundy of his legal authority to rule favorably on behalf of their clients. The first hurdle was to convince the judge their clients were persons and the writ should be confirmed.

Lambertson began the trial believing Judge Dundy had legal authority to dismiss the case because the law considered Native Americans to be "wards of the government," not "persons."[3] Therefore, because the relators were not persons under the law, they had no standing or right to appear in court and the writ should be quashed. As Lambertson prepared for the second day of the trial, he likely had some doubt in his mind, because Judge Dundy had demonstrated his willingness to listen to the relators' witnesses. When Lambertson questioned Standing Bear's right to testify, Judge Dundy possibly surprised him with the reply, "Anybody can be sworn, this court recognizes no distinction on account of race, color or previous condition."[4] As the second day of the trial was about to begin, Lambertson likely thought this was not an open-and-shut case.

### Court Convened (May 2, 1879)

On Friday May 2, 1879, the second day of the trial began. Judge Dundy entered the courtroom at 10:00 a.m. Tibbles reported that "as on the day previous there was a large number of ladies and leading citizens present all deeply interested in behalf of the Poncas."[5]

### Timeline—Day 2

Based upon the accounts of the trial given in the *Omaha Daily Herald*, Webster spoke for approximately three hours, Lambertson spoke for approximately three hours, Poppleton spoke for just over two hours, and Standing Bear spoke for nearly thirty minutes. The following is an approximate timeline of the second day of the trial:

10:00 a.m. Court convened.
  Webster spoke for two hours.[6]
12:00 p.m. Court recessed.
1:30 p.m. Court re-convened.
  Webster spoke "about an hour more."[7]
2:30 p.m. Lambertson spoke "for nearly three hours."[8]
5:30 p.m. Court recessed.
7:30 p.m. Court re-convened.
  Poppleton spoke "for over two hours."[9]
9:30 p.m. Poppleton concludes.[10]
10:00 p.m. Standing Bear closed his speech at "nearly 10 o'clock"[11]

### Closing Argument of John L. Webster

The May 3, 1879, edition of the *Omaha Daily Herald* reported that Webster spoke for two hours, stopping at twelve o'clock when court recessed. At 1:30 p.m. court reconvened, and Webster spoke for about an hour more.[12]

During his three-hour discourse, Webster attempted to convince the judge that the writ should be confirmed and the relators released from the hands of the government. To do so, he laid out a series of arguments beginning with a matter-of-fact statement that the Omaha tribe had "the right to invite their friends (i.e., Standing Bear and his companions) to dwell with them and share the land . . . for their title is good, they have the use and occupancy in which they cannot be disturbed."[13] Webster believed there was no legal authority to prevent Standing Bear from staying with his cousins, or going back on his own land in the Niobrara River valley.

His argument was founded upon his belief that the rights of Native Americans were "acknowledged when this continent was first discovered. They are based upon great principles which never change. They are like the law of nations. The government cannot change them."[14]

Webster quoted a letter written in 1805 to an Indian chief by Thomas Jefferson in which the president declared, "these lands can never go from you, but when you wish to sell." Webster concurred saying the government cannot take their lands "from them by treaty or otherwise, without their free consent."[15]

Building upon this argument, Webster attacked what he considered to be a misinterpretation of the Doctrine of Discovery:

> The principle accepted by all European nations who had made discoveries on this continent, was that it gave them no absolute authority over the inhabitants who occupied the discovered countries or ownership of the soil against the original occupants, but it gave them a title good against other European claimants. That was all there was in a title by discovery! Did the landing of a few whites upon the shores of the Atlantic give them a title to the lands which the Poncas then owned and occupied. No such claim as this has ever been made. *Discovery only gave a title to lands which were unoccupied.*[16]

In his next argument, Webster stated that he believed Indian tribes had been considered by the government as independent nations, saying that the government "acknowledged their national character in making treaties with them. They had their own government and their own laws . . . these Omaha and Poncas are not savages nor wanderers. They cultivate the soil, live in houses, and support themselves."[17]

Tibbles reported that Webster quoted "many authoritative sources that Indian Tribes maintaining their organization as such were separate and independent nations and had all the rights and privileges of such except what they had relinquished by special treaty stipulations."[18]

Webster said it naturally followed from this line of thinking:

> If these Indians belonged to the Ponca tribe and their tribal relations were unbroken that they had a right as an independent nation to go back to their land which they still owned, or the Omaha tribe had a right to receive them into their nation, and there was no power in the government of the United States to interfere.[19]

Webster provided Judge Dundy authority upon which he could base his ruling, the newly passed Fourteenth Amendment to the United States Constitution. He quoted Section 1 thereof:

> All persons born or naturalized in the United States, and subject to the jurisdiction thereof are citizens of the United States and of the state wherein they reside. No state shall make or enforce any law which shall abridge the privileges or immunities of citizens of the United States; nor shall any state deprive any person of life, liberty or property, without due process of law; nor deny to any person within its jurisdiction the equal protection of the laws.[20]

Webster told the court that when an Indian severed his tribal relations, he stopped his allegiance to his tribal chiefs and thereby became a citizen of the United States. He quoted from a report made by the Senate Judiciary Committee in 1870: "It is pertinent to say, in concluding this report, that treaty relations can properly exist with Indian tribes or nations only, and that, when the members of a tribe are scattered, they are merged in the mass of our people, and become equally subject to the jurisdiction of the United States."[21]

Webster briefly discussed the plight of Standing Bear and the Ponca people and the great deprivations and sufferings they had endured in being taken against their will by the military, with no justifiable reason under the law. The Poncas had committed no crime against the government or any white settlers. By frequently referring to the Poncas as "prisoners of war" and at the same time calling them "persons" and "citizens," Webster intended to emphasize to the court the injustice of their arrest and imprisonment. He concluded his remarks with a passionate plea for freedom:

> They have fled with their wives and children from this pestilential prison, and now ask the protection of the court. They say we are men; we have a right to go where we please. We are citizens of the United States. In the words of Frederick Douglas, *a man belongs to himself.* His hands are his own, his feet are his own, his body is his own, and they will remain his until you storm the citadel of heaven, and wrest from the bosom of God, man's title deed to himself.[22]

Webster sat down. He had given a passionate argument backed by authoritative sources. He had done his job in laying the foundation for his clients to be freed. Tibbles reported that Webster's words were "especially brilliant and powerful and made a deep impression on all present."[23]

### Closing Argument of Genio M. Lambertson

United States District Attorney Lambertson found himself sandwiched between two experienced and eloquent lawyers who quoted not only from legal sources, but also from the writings of ancient philosophers, to make their arguments. Despite the fact a jury would not decide this case, Lambertson was likely aware that opposing counsel was offering to the court the recently adopted Fourteenth Amendment. This was something the judge could rely upon as authority in deciding the case. As Webster concluded his remarks, Judge Dundy directed Lambertson to make his closing argument.

At approximately 2:30 p.m. Lambertson rose to speak. Tibbles reported that he "spoke for nearly three hours." He began with an unusual tribute to the "generosity" of opposing counsel "coming to the assistance of these poor people, prisoners and friendless in a strange land."[24]

The *Omaha Daily Herald* did not give as much coverage to Lambertson's closing argument, especially in light of the coverage given to the arguments made by Webster and Poppleton. However, the May 3, 1879, edition of the newspaper included a concise summary of the major points Lambertson made to the court: (1) an Indian has no standing to come into the court because he is not a person or a citizen, therefore not entitled to a writ of habeas corpus; (2) Indian tribes are not independent, but dependent communities, based upon the Doctrine of Discovery expounded by Justice Marshall; and (3) Judge Taney's decision in the Dred Scott case should be binding on this court because it ruled that Scott could not sue in federal court as he was not a person or a citizen of the United States.[25]

Lambertson entered into a lengthy discussion of the writ of habeas corpus and restated his belief that the court did not have any power to adjudicate this matter saying:

> To come within the jurisdiction of the court, the complainants' must be either a foreign subject or a citizen of one of the states, or the case must arise under the laws of the United States, the constitution or treaties. The complainants were not citizens or subjects of a foreign state, and they were not citizens of the United States. The Fourteenth Amendment did not apply to them, for the complainants had not dissolved their tribal relations.[26]

It can be inferred from Judge Dundy's language in his decision that Lambertson also spent considerable time defending the government's decision to arrest the relators for leaving Indian Territory without government permission, noting that Lambertson denied that "the Relators had withdrawn and severed, for all time, their connection with the tribe to which they belonged."[27]

Judge Dundy stated in his opinion that "the district attorney has supported his theory with an argument of great ingenuity and much ability."[28]

It was after 5:30 p.m. when the district attorney took his seat. Judge Dundy had allocated only two days for the trial because he had other business waiting for him in Lincoln. He adjourned the proceedings for supper.[29]

### Closing Argument of Andrew J. Poppleton

After the court reconvened for an unusual evening session, Judge Dundy directed Andrew J. Poppleton to deliver his closing argument. It was 7:30 p.m. Toward the end of his life, Poppleton recalled how that moment affected him:

> Without fee or reward or any hope or promise of compensation, Mr. Webster and myself entered upon this work and espoused the cause of the Indians. The hearing took place before District Court Judge Dundy

at Omaha. I delivered my argument upon that case in the evening in the large court room of the Federal Building on the corner of Dodge and Fifteenth Streets. There were present in addition to the court and its officers, an audience taxing the fine capacity of the room, including General Crook and other officers under his command, and many ladies. I have spoken to larger audiences, but I think never to one more intelligent and sympathetic, and in looking back I cannot now recall any two hours work of my life with which I feel better satisfied.[30]

Poppleton's wife, Caroline, was likely among the "many ladies" present in the courtroom that evening to listen and support her husband in the most historic case of his distinguished career.

The *Omaha Daily Herald* allocated the largest number of columns for the closing argument of Andrew Poppleton, more than for the closing arguments of Webster and Lambertson combined. The May 4, 1879, headline read:

## A PLEA FOR THE PONCAS

The Argument of Hon A. J. Poppleton
to the Habeas Corpus Case

What the Great Writ of Liberty
Really Means

It Applies to Every Human Being
on the Face of the Earth
How the Power of Forty Millions
of People is used to Crush
a Few Helpless Indians

A Powerful Appeal for the Down
Trodden, who for Two Hundred Years
Have had None
to Defend Them

Interesting Scenes and Incidents in the Court Room

Tibbles began his report on Poppleton's closing argument by saying the audience in the courtroom "listened with breathless attention to every word.... From the very start it was a masterly speech, but the latter portion was intensely thrilling and powerful."[31] Poppleton began his closing argument by saying:

> May it please the Court. I suppose it would be impossible for counsel under any circumstances to approach a case of this character without a feeling of oppression at its magnitude and the consequences involved in it.... It is intensified in this case by the fact that I am to appear here on behalf of a feeble remnant of a class of beings who seem, for two or three hundred years to have had no friends and to have never had any rights.[32]

Poppleton questioned Lambertson's argument against the relators' application for a writ of habeas corpus, saying: "I confess I have been somewhat surprised as to the character of the argument made here. What is it in effect, is that these relators have no right whatever, not even the right of petition, not even the right to the protection of their liberty. What is the reason in that?"[33]

Poppleton asked why the government didn't offer concrete evidence of a particular law giving them the right to remove the Poncas to Indian Territory. He also asked why the government did not disclose any treaty broken by the Poncas to justify its actions. After all, Poppleton said, the burden of proof was on the government:

> If there is any contract, any agreement of any description whatever which justifies the government in trying to hold these people in the Indian Territory, that contract lies in its possession, and had something like a month to prepare for this hearing and it should have produced it here, to show to the Court some premise and some reason why the Indians are sought to be held.[34]

He stayed in this line of argument for a few minutes, as he wondered aloud how the district attorney could make the assertion that the Poncas were without any rights. He said: "Our government has gone and made treaties with them in which the government has undertaken to guarantee them certain rights, certain lands and certain privileges in connection with these lands, and now to turn back on those guarantees is a most infamous act, because it is treachery on the part of power as against weakness."[35]

Poppleton discussed the erroneous Dred Scott decision and gratefully acknowledged that it had been rectified by the Fourteenth Amendment. He noted, however, that during that struggle, the writ of habeas corpus was employed successfully on behalf of fugitive slaves. At the same time, Poppleton expressed his "feeling of humiliation when the great government of the United States comes here with no better argument than that these Indians have no rights whatsoever."[36]

Then Poppleton told the court he believed Lambertson's suggestion that the Indians lost all their rights via the Indian Appropriation Act of 1871 was wrong, saying: "Your Honor may not have noticed one of the significant provisions of that Act which said clearly that it should not be construed as abrogating any treaty theretofore entered into with any Indian Tribe." Poppleton pointed to a specific clause in the 1858 Ponca Treaty which said a certain tract of land near the Niobrara River is "reserved for the future home of said Indians" and the government agreed to "protect these Indians in possession of this tract of land reserved for their future home, and their persons and property thereon."[37]

In Poppleton's point of view, Lambertson erred when he told the court that the government had "given" the Poncas tools, houses and plows, when, in effect, this was not a gift but "consideration" for the relinquishment of their rights to certain land they were ceding to the government. It was a contractual arrangement, Poppleton argued, that did not authorize the government to unilaterally change the terms of the treaty when the Poncas had not broken its end of the bargain.[38]

Poppleton spent a considerable portion of his time analyzing the 1858 and 1865 Ponca treaties and promises made to the tribe. He also discussed the terrible injustice done to the Poncas by the government's 1868 Fort Laramie Treaty with the Sioux, saying: "One thing the government undertook to do, at any rate, was to give away the rights of the Poncas north of the Niobrara to the Sioux. Will any man stand here and contend there is any good faith in that, any honor in that? Is there any justice in that?"[39]

Poppleton's reputation as a passionate trial lawyer was displayed frequently in his two hours before the court, as these words demonstrate:

I tell your Honor it is an outrage—and the word outrage doesn't express it—it is an infamy difficult to grasp. . . . Is it possible that this great government, standing here dealing with this feeble remnant of a once powerful nation, claims the right to place them in a condition which is to them worse that slaves, without a syllable of law; without a syllable or contract or treaty? I don't believe, if your Honor please, that the courts will allow this; that they will agree to the proposition that these people are wild beasts; that they have no status in the courts. The argument of the gentleman representing the government comes to that—they are simply wild beasts.[40]

That led Poppleton into a discussion on "this Great Writ that for five hundred years has been the shield and protection of individual liberty until it has made every man a sovereign the world over." He strongly believed that the prisoners had the right to petition the court for a writ of habeas corpus to

Protect themselves against lawless violence because everything in this country not done by law is lawless violence. In looking over judicial decisions I found this language: *"No human being in this country can exercise any kind of public authority which is not conferred by law. In the United States it must be given by the express words of a written statute. Whatever is not given is withheld and the exercise of it is positively prohibited."* If there is any power in the military to hold these people, it must be under a positive statute. I protest against the power of the military to arrest them, and I think the military itself has a right to protest. (emphasis added)[41]

Just as Poppleton was returning to a brief discussion of the use of the writ for the benefit of a fugitive slave, a dramatic moment occurred in the courtroom. District Attorney Lambertson abruptly interrupted Poppleton's speech with a question:

**Lambertson:**  After the Dred Scott decision, did a slave ever invoke the Writ in a Federal Court?

**Poppleton:**  No. After that there probably was no opportunity to invoke it. It was repeatedly invoked before . . . In this country now, Judge Taney's decision has gone out of date, and I don't see how it is possible to bring the

Indians under any disability under the Fourteenth
Amendment, unless some express laws can be
produced to that effect.[42]

Lambertson sat down. Toward the end of his argument, Poppleton restated
something Standing Bear had said in court that deeply affected him: "During
the sixty days I was coming from the Indian Territory to the Omaha agency
I carried the bones of my boy in a box, and I have got them now. It is my
sacred desire, it is my absorbing purpose, it is my highest aspiration to carry
the ashes of that boy and bury them where in his last hours he wished to
be buried."[43] Poppleton paused. He looked at Standing Bear and said in
summation:

> That man not a human being? Who of us all would have done it? Look
> around this city and state and find, if you can, the man who has gathered
> up the ashes of his dead son, wandered for sixty days through a strange
> country without guide or compass, aided by the sun and stars only, that
> the bones of his son may be buried in the land of their birth. No! It is a
> libel upon religion; it is libel upon missionaries who sacrifice so much
> and risk their lives in order to take to these Indians that gospel which
> Christ proclaimed to all the wide earth, to say that these are not human
> beings. But if they are human beings they cannot be barred from the
> right to this Writ.[44]

Poppleton finished. It was nearly 9:30 p.m.[45] Court adjourned. But Judge
Dundy did not rise and leave the courtroom. He remained on the bench.
The evening was not over.

# 15

## Standing Bear's Historic Speech

It was 9:30 p.m. on Friday, May 2, 1879. The three attorneys had finished their closing arguments, after speaking collectively for over eight hours. Court was adjourned. For all intents and purposes the trial was over. Everyone was waiting for the U.S. marshal to call out "All rise" as the judge left the courtroom. But Judge Dundy did not leave. Instead, he motioned Standing Bear to speak.[1] Bright Eyes stood ready to interpret his words.

Standing Bear likely realized the importance of the opportunity afforded him by Judge Dundy, and wanted the most accurate and trustworthy person to translate his words. He would have been most comfortable with his cousin Bright Eyes because she had complete knowledge of his story as a result of (1) the three days he had lived in her home (March 1877); (2) the three days she and her father stayed with the Poncas near Columbus, Nebraska, on their forced march (May 1877); and (3) the two weeks he stayed on the Omaha reservation prior to his arrest (March 1879). In addition, she was fluent in the Ponca and English languages.

---

**Bright Eyes (1854–1903)**

Susette LaFlesche (*Inshta-Theamba*) known as "Bright Eyes," was a cousin of Standing Bear and a member of the Omaha Tribe. She was born in Bellevue, Nebraska, in 1854, the daughter of Iron Eye (Joseph LaFlesche), chief of the Omaha Tribe, and Mary Gale LaFlesche. Her grandfather, John Gale, was a surgeon in the U.S. Army. Bright Eyes learned to read and write English while attending the Presbyterian Mission Boarding Day School located on her tribal land near Decatur, Nebraska. She attended the prestigious Elizabeth Institute for Young Ladies in New Jersey. Upon graduation in 1875, she became a teacher in the Omaha Agency School.[2] Lieutenant Bourke referred to her as "an Omaha Indian lady of excellent attainments and bright intellect."[3]

---

### Standing Bear Desires to Speak

When he had been called to the witness stand on the first day of the trial, Standing Bear became frustrated as the lawyers on both sides asked him leading questions and interrupted his answers. As grateful as he was for the effort his lawyers expended on his behalf, Standing Bear wanted an opportunity to speak. In that way, he believed the judge could hear all of the facts regarding the injustice, sufferings, and deaths his people had endured. He wanted the judge to know what the government had done to his people. He wanted to tell his own story.

Judge Dundy had no legal precedent to guide him in deciding whether to grant Standing Bear's request. There is no written evidence as to whether Judge Dundy gave prior notice to the three lawyers of his decision to allow Standing Bear to speak at the end of the trial. However, one can assume he did give prior notice, because there is no evidence that any of the attorneys raised an objection.

A special opportunity was being afforded to a special man.

The moment had arrived.

### The Historic Moment

Tibbles reported that after Poppleton sat down "Judge Dundy said that Standing Bear had made a request to address the court. He supposed that to grant such a request would be entirely unprecedented, but he should grant the request. He supposed that it was the first time in the history of the country that an Indian ever addressed a court."[4]

Rising from where he had been sitting, Standing Bear turned sideways, half-facing the audience and half-facing the judge. Bright Eyes came near him to interpret his words. Holding his red blanket with his left hand, he extended his right hand outward, and remained like that for a few moments. Everyone had their eyes fixed on him wondering if the moment was too emotional for him, or if he was tired due to the lateness of evening and the close air in the room. Slowly he looked directly at Judge Dundy and began to speak:

I see a great many of you here.
I think a great many are my friends.
Where do you think I came from?
From the water? From the woods?

God made me, just as he made all of you, and
God put me on my land.

But a man I did not know came and
ordered me to leave my land.
I objected.
I looked around for a friend to help me,
but there was none.

Now I have found someone (casting his eyes towards his attorneys)
and it makes me glad.[5]

Standing Bear then told the story of the Poncas forced move to Indian
Territory and the death of 158 of his people. He said he did not want to die
there. He came away to save his wife, his children, his friends. He wanted to
go home, to bury the bones of his dead son, and to live out the remainder of
his life in the land of his fathers. He never tried to hurt a white man. Once
when out hunting, he found an American soldier on the prairie, almost
frozen. He took him home, made him warm, and fed him until he could go
away.[6] Then Standing Bear raised his hand to the perpendicular and held
it there saying:

That hand is not the color of yours.
But if I pierce it, I shall feel pain.
If you pierce your hand, you also feel pain.
The blood that will flow from mine, will be
the same color as yours.
**I AM A MAN.**
The same God made us both.[7]

The courtroom was silent. Everyone listened intently as Standing Bear
paused, then turning towards an open window in the courtroom and looking
up into the evening sky, Standing Bear then spoke metaphorically:

I seem to stand on the bank of a river.
My wife and little girl are beside me.

In front the river is wide and impassable, and behind are
    perpendicular cliffs.
No man of my race ever stood there before.
There is no tradition to guide me.

A flood has begun to rise around us.
I look despairingly at the great cliffs.
I see a steep, stony way leading upward.
I grasp the hand of my child and my wife follows.
I lead the way up the sharp rocks, while the waters rise
behind us.

Finally, I see a rift in the rocks, and
I feel the prairie breeze strike my cheek.
I turn to my wife and child with a shout that we are saved. We will
    return to the Swift Running Water that pours down between the
    green islands.

There are the graves of my fathers.
There again we will pitch our tipi and build our fires.

**But a man bars the passage**!
He is a thousand times more powerful than I.
Behind him, I see soldiers as numerous as leaves on trees.
They will obey that man's orders.
I too must obey his orders.
If he says that I cannot pass, I cannot.
The long struggle will have been in vain. My wife and child and I must
    return and sink beneath the flood. We are weak and faint and sick.
    I cannot fight.

Looking directly at Judge Dundy, Standing Bear said:

**You are that man!**[8]

Standing Bear sat down.

### Reaction in the Courtroom

Tibbles reported that "it was nearly 10 o'clock when Standing Bear closed his speech, which was greeted with a round of applause. The ladies pressed up around him to shake hands with him."[9] Tibbles saw raw emotion on the faces of Judge Dundy, General Crook, and others.

Tibbles reported that "Judge Dundy said he would take the case under advisement and give his decision hereafter." Then the judge left the bench.[10]

The local and national reporters hurried outside to chronicle the story for their readers. The lawyers, clergy, civic leaders, and general public walked down the three flights of stairs and out into the streets of downtown Omaha, tired, hot, and likely emotionally drained. They had just witnessed history being made.

The soldiers loaded Standing Bear and the other Poncas onto wagons for the four-mile trip back to Fort Omaha. They entered the courtroom as prisoners; they left as prisoners. Whether they would ever be free again was out of their control.

One man would decide that question. They would have to wait ten days for his decision.

### Reflection on Standing Bear's Eloquence

Standing Bear was a gifted speaker who employed words and images to convey his thoughts in a clear, poetic, and eloquent way. The words attributed to him in his various recorded speeches should not be called into question as being invented by an interpreter or a reporter because three different interpreters (Charles Morgan, William Hamilton, and Bright Eyes) and two different reporters (Thomas Tibbles and Lt. John G. Bourke) at different times in 1879 (March 30, March 31, May 1, and May 2) and at different locations (his prison tent at Fort Omaha, General Crook's office, and the federal courthouse) proved this:

1. Charles Morgan interpreted Standing Bear's remarks, as reported by Thomas Tibbles on March 30, 1879, in his prison tent at Fort Omaha (chapter 10).
2. Charles Morgan again interpreted Standing Bear's remarks as reported by Lt. John Bourke on March 31, 1879, in General Crook's office (chapter 10).

3. William Hamilton interpreted Standing Bear's testimony during the trial on May 1, 1879, as reported by Tibbles (chapter 13).

4. Bright Eyes interpreted Standing Bear's historic speech on May 2, 1879, as reported by Thomas Tibbles (chapter 15).

5. All three interpreters and both reporters reflect the same poetic beauty and spirit of Standing Bear.

The lasting effect of Standing Bear's historic courtroom speech is further confirmed in a statement made in 1915 by Caroline L. Poppleton, wife of Andrew Poppleton, when she recalled the powerful words Standing Bear spoke in her home on May 20, 1879: "*I believe I told you in the courtroom that God made me and that I was a man.*" Standing Bear's words, spoken "out of the wealth of his human soul, and out of the fullness of his manly heart," remained in her memory thirty-six years later.[11]

# 16

## A Time for Waiting

For the next ten days, everyone involved in the case waited for Judge Elmer S. Dundy to render his decision.

### The Prisoners

Standing Bear and his companions waited on the grounds of Fort Omaha, prisoners of the United States government. They must have wondered what the future held for them:

Would they be allowed to go home?
Would they ever be allowed to live their lives and raise their children as they desired?
Would they be forced to go back to a land they found without hope, full of sickness and death?

Standing Bear and his wife must also have wondered whether they would be allowed to bury the bones of their beloved son, Bear Shield. They loved him and wanted above all else to be able to fulfill his dying wish—to be buried in the soil of his ancestors so as to walk in the afterlife in the comfort of his people, not alone.

In a letter dated May 8, 1879, Lieutenant Carpenter, the officer who arrested Standing Bear and brought him and the other Poncas to Fort Omaha, described his prisoners after nearly two months under his charge:

From my personal knowledge of these people while under my charge, I consider them further advanced in civilization than any other tribe west of the Mississippi, with the single exception of the Omahas, to whom they are related by the bond of common origin. The men are industrious and willing to work, at anything they can find to do. The children conduct themselves well, and the women are modest in their demeanor and neat in appearance and domestic habits.[1]

### Thomas Tibbles

Tibbles went back to work at his desk in the offices of the *Omaha Daily Herald*, writing the events of the trial for his readers in Omaha that would be picked up by newspapers throughout America. *Tibbles was the scribe of history.* He wrote a record of these two historic days from notes he made while sitting behind the relators' table. He described the timing of what happened in the courtroom, the substance of the questioning of witnesses, the objections raised by the lawyers, the comments of the judge to the objections raised, and the closing arguments made by the three lawyers. He also gave us a complete record of Standing Bear's memorable speech.

### Judge Elmer Dundy

Judge Dundy spent the week pondering the facts of the case and the arguments he had heard. He researched statutes, treaties, and the historic relationship the Poncas had with the government. The judge was aware he would be criticized whichever way he ruled, saying: "As the matter furnishes so much valuable material for discussion, and so much food for reflection, I shall try to present it as viewed from my own standpoint, without reference to consequences or criticisms, which, though not specially invited, will be sure to follow."[2]

If he ruled in favor of the relators, Judge Dundy would be criticized by white settlers who wanted the land cleared of Native Americans to move onto it themselves, and by the government and military who wanted to preserve the reservation system in Indian Territory. At the same time, if he ruled in favor of the government an outcry of injustice would likely be directed at him from the media, clergy, and supporters of Native American reform.

### Three Distinguished Lawyers

Webster, Poppleton, and Lambertson went about their legal work as usual. Each lawyer in his own way possibly wondered if he should have called another witness, asked another question, raised another objection, included just one more point in his closing argument, or maybe even wished he had left something unsaid. It is not unusual for lawyers to rehash a case after it is over, sometimes even second-guessing themselves. But at some point every trial lawyer has to let the matter rest, knowing he or she did the best they could at the time and under the circumstances. Hindsight never won a case.

In 1832, the year George Catlin came to the Ponca village to study their culture and paint their portraits, a French political scientist, Alexis de Toc-queville, spent nine months on the East Coast observing the workings of the American democracy and questioning how this young democracy was functioning. The conclusion he reached is of interest because of the crucial role lawyers played in the United States at that time. Alexis de Tocqueville wrote: "In visiting the Americans and studying their laws, we perceive that the authority they have entrusted to members of the legal profession, and the influence which these individuals exercise in the government, is the most powerful existing security against the excesses of democracy."[3]

Webster, Poppleton, and Lambertson were admirable in their represen-tation of their clients in unprecedented circumstances. They were forced to be creative in questioning and cross-examining witnesses, in making objections, and most especially in delivering their closing arguments. They had no case law to rely upon as precedent to support their positions.

These three distinguished Nebraska lawyers stood before the court in a place no other lawyer had ever stood in the history of American jurispru-dence. No other lawyer anywhere in the United States, not in Boston, St. Louis, New York, Chicago, or any other city, had ever stood in a federal courtroom to argue such a case.

Lambertson had no choice but to participate in this case. He was assigned to represent the government. It was his duty as the district attorney. If he deserves any criticism, it would fall on his failure to realize the potential ramifications the Fourteenth Amendment to the Constitution could have on the case.

Webster and Poppleton on the other hand, did have a choice. They could have said "no" to Thomas Tibbles. They could have told him he was asking something no experienced lawyer would want to spend time on, especially when they were asked to do it for free. After all, there were fifty-seven other lawyers in Omaha at the time. They could have simply told Tibbles to find someone else. Instead they agreed to take the case while understanding the challenge presented to them, as Poppleton later wrote: "The question of whether the writ would lie on behalf of a tribal Indian and also whether the United States had any lawful power by its soldiery to remove him were wholly new and of vast importance. Without fee or reward or any hope or promise of compensation, Mr. Webster and myself entered upon this work and espoused the cause of the Indians."[4]

*Summary*

As the participants in the trial waited for Judge Dundy to issue his ruling, some may have wondered what effect the Fourteenth Amendment would have on the outcome. Others may have speculated on what impact Standing Bear's dramatic speech could have on the decision. All were anxious to hear from Judge Dundy.

None of the three lawyers, or the judge, or any other person sitting in the courtroom those two days in May 1879 were prepared for the effect this man would have on them as they listened to him speak and observed his dignity, eloquence, and passion. Standing Bear had a nobility about himself, a commanding presence, similar to Ponca Chief Smoke Maker (Shu-de-ga-xe), whom George Catlin had come to know and paint visiting the Ponca Tribe in 1832.

No one captured the attention of those in the audience more than Standing Bear. His very presence towered above everyone else in the courtroom. He could not be ignored. His cause could not be dismissed. A decision must be made.

Standing Bear knew he was a person, a human being, made by God. He did not need a judge to tell him that. But he knew that his people and all Native Americans needed the judge to say it.

Justice cried out for it to be said.
   The time had come for it to be said.
   America needed to hear it.

# 17

## The Court's Decision

The headline on the front page of the May 13, 1879 edition of the *Omaha Daily Herald* captured the essence of Judge Elmer S. Dundy's historic decision rendered the previous day.[1]

### STANDING BEAR VICTORY

Judge Dundy Issues an Order
Releasing the Ponca Indians.

A Decision Far Reaching In Its Effects

There is no Law for Using the Military
To Force Indians from one
Place to Another

The Indian Ring is Shorn of its Power

An Indian has Some Rights Which
The Courts will Protect

*United States ex rel. Standing Bear v. George Crook*, 5 Dill. 453, 25 F. Cas. 695, was reported in the *Circuit Court Reports for Cases Determined in the United States Circuit Courts for the Eighth Circuit*, officially certified by John F. Dillon.[2]

### Standing Bear Was Present in the Courtroom

Standing Bear and others were present in the federal courthouse in Omaha on May 12, 1879, to hear Judge Dundy read his decision. A reporter from the *St. Louis Republican* newspaper wrote: "Standing Bear is a man of rare ability for an Indian, and during the reading of the Court's opinion today, he was present with his handsome wife, Susette, and others of his tribe, and at the close of the reading they received their liberty and congratulations of friends with feelings of joy."[3]

It is probable that Webster, Poppleton, and Bright Eyes were also present in the courtroom to hear the decision. Judge Dundy had nothing in case law to guide him in these matters. He was setting precedents that would guide judges in the future: (1) by granting Standing Bear and the Ponca prisoners their day in court when he accepted their application for the writ; (2) by allowing Standing Bear to testify as a witness in the trial; and (3) by granting Standing Bear the privilege of addressing the court at the end of the trial. Judge Dundy fully understood the historic nature of the case. So permitting these interested parties to be present in the courtroom to hear the ruling would have been appropriate. In addition, Bright Eyes testified before the Senate Select Committee on February 13, 1880, that she "was in Omaha at the time."[4]

### Opening Remarks of Judge Dundy

Judge Dundy began his opening remarks by saying: "During the fifteen years in which I have been engaged in administering the laws of my country, I have never been called upon to hear or decide a case that appealed so strongly to my sympathy as the one now under consideration."[5]

He then contrasted the two parties represented in the courtroom:

On the one side, we have a few remnants of a once numerous and powerful, but now weak, insignificant, unlettered and generally despised race; on the other, we have the representatives of one of the most powerful, most enlightened, and most Christianized nations of modern times ... We have the representatives of this wasted race coming into this national tribunal of ours, asking for justice and liberty to enable them to adopt our boasted civilization, and to pursue the arts of peace ... and ... we have this magnificent, if not magnanimous government resisting this application with the determination of sending these people back to the country which is to them less desirable than perpetual imprisonment in their own native land.[6]

Judge Dundy mirrored some of Poppleton's passionate words spoken at the conclusion of his closing argument:

| ANDREW POPPLETON | JUDGE DUNDY |
|---|---|
| "earliest possessors of this soil" | "once numerous and powerful race" |
| "through a strange country" | "a country . . . less desirable" |
| "land of their birth" | "their own native land" |
| "gospel of Christ" | "Christianized nations" |
| "human beings" | "people" |

Following a compliment "to the heart and mind of the brave and distinguished officer who is made respondent herein" (General George Crook), Judge Dundy concluded his opening remarks by acknowledging his responsibility in making this landmark decision:

> In a country where liberty is regulated by law, something more satisfactory and enduring than mere sympathy must furnish and constitute the rule and basis of judicial action. It follows that this case must be examined and decided on principles of law, and that unless the Relators are entitled to their discharge under the constitution or laws of the United States, or some treaty made pursuant thereto, they must be remanded to the custody of the officer who caused their arrest, to be returned to Indian Territory, which they left without the consent of the government.[7]

### Confirmation of the Process

Judge Dundy described how this matter came before the court. He listed the date when the relators made application for a writ of habeas corpus, the date he issued the writ, the date service was made upon General Crook, and its return. He declared that all steps in the process had been properly executed.

### Issue One: Does This Court Have Jurisdiction to Issue the Writ of Habeas Corpus and Hear the Case

Judge Dundy proceeded to discuss the first issue before the court: jurisdiction. The district attorney raised the question of whether this court had jurisdiction to issue the writ on behalf of these relators, much less hold a hearing regarding the matter.

After referencing Lambertson's initial concern, Judge Dundy immediately said, "I am of the opinion that his premises are erroneous, and his conclusions, therefore, wrong and unjust." He did not think "it necessary to examine the English laws regulating the suing out of the writ," saying instead that "this only proves that the laws of a limited monarchy are sometimes less wise and humane that the laws of our own republic."[8]

Citing sections 751–53 of the Revised Statutes, Judge Dundy said, "when a person is in custody or deprived of his liberty under color of authority of the United States, or in violation of the constitution or laws or treaties of the United States, the Federal Judges have jurisdiction, and the Writ can properly issue."[9]

Are the relators therefore entitled to the writ, the judge queried? Answering his own question in light of these statutes, Judge Dundy said, "They certainly are, because they are in custody of a federal officer under color of authority of the United States; and because they are restrained of liberty in violation of a provision of their treaty."[10] Judge Dundy earlier referenced the Treaty of 1858, in which the government guaranteed the Poncas a certain tract of land near the Niobrara River for their permanent home.

Addressing the requirement in the Habeas Corpus Act of 1867 that an applicant must be "persons" or "parties" to be entitled to the writ, Judge Dundy said:

It nowhere describes them as *citizens*, nor is citizenship in any way or place made a qualification for suing out the Writ, and in the absence of express provision or necessary implication which would require the interpretation contended for by the District Attorney, I should not feel justified in giving the words *person* and *party* such a narrow construction.[11]

Judge Dundy employed a common principle in interpretation of specific words, saying that "the most natural, and therefore most reasonable way is to attach the same meaning to *words and phrases* when found in a statute that is attached to them when and where found in general use." Quoting attorney Webster in his description of a person "as a living soul; a self-conscious being; a moral agent; especially a living human being; a man, woman or child; an individual of the human race," Judge Dundy agreed that "this is comprehensive enough, it would seem, to include even an Indian." He then made a precedent-setting statement: "I must hold, then, that *Indians*, and consequently the Relators, are *persons*, such as are described by and included within the laws before quoted."[12]

The second element of the issue the district attorney had raised was whether a federal court was the proper forum to hear the Relators' application for a writ, since it had never been heard in any federal court. "This is a *non sequitur*." Judge Dundy concluded, "I confess I do not know of another instance where this has been done, but I can also say that the occasion for it perhaps has never before been so great."[13]

*Note*: The Latin term *non sequitur* means "it does not follow." That is, the inference does not follow from the argument.[14]

Complimenting the Relators for seeking a peaceful redress of their grievances in this tribunal rather than resorting to armed resistance, Judge Dundy said that this tribunal "is the only one into which they can lawfully go for deliverance"; and it was irrelevant that "none of their ancestors ever sought relief thereunder."[15]

Judge Dundy concluded his remarks on this first issue, saying: "It would indeed be a sad commentary on the justice and impartiality of our laws to hold that Indians, though natives of our own country, cannot test the validity of an alleged illegal imprisonment in this matter, as well as a subject of a foreign government who may happen to be sojourning this county."[16]

### Issue Two: Does an Indian Possess the Right of Expatriation

Ruling that the relators qualified as "persons" to make an application for a writ of habeas corpus, and that this federal court was the proper forum to hear it, Judge Dundy moved on to what he considered to be "a question of much greater importance . . . which when determined, will be decisive of this whole controversy . . . the right of the government to arrest and hold the Relators for a time, for the purpose of being returned to a point in the Indian Territory from which it is alleged the Indians escaped."[17]

In deciding this second issue, Judge Dundy stated that he reviewed the government policies employed with the Ponca Tribe, including the Treaties of 1858 and 1865. He recognized the fact that the Poncas "have been at peace with the government, and have remained the steadfast friends of the whites, for many years; they lived peaceably upon the land and in the country, they claimed and called their own."[18] He cited the government's

Treaty of 1868 with the Lakota Sioux in which the Poncas' guaranteed land was taken from them "without consultation with, or knowledge or consent on the part of, the Ponca tribe of Indians."[19]

Judge Dundy recalled the testimony of Standing Bear in which he described the effects the move to Indian Territory had on his people, including severe illness and death. It was the reason he gave for his decision "to leave Indian Territory and return to his own home." Then, something quite remarkable happened. Judge Dundy inserted in his decision an actual quote that Standing Bear made on the witness stand that all he wanted "was to live and die in peace and be buried with his fathers."[20]

Judge Dundy proceeded to summarize the time, place, and intent of the relators at the moment the military arrested them on March 25, 1879. He described Standing Bear's testimony that he and his companions left the reservation in Indian Territory with the intent to sever their ties to their tribe forever, and to bury the bones of his dead son in his native land. Judge Dundy concluded that "such instances of parental affection, and such love of home and native land, may be heathen in origin, but it seems to me that they are not unlike Christian in principle."[21]

Judge Dundy then asked the key question: "whether an Indian can withdraw from his tribe, sever his tribal relation therewith, and terminate his allegiance thereto, for the purpose of making an independent living and adopting our own civilization?"[22]

Quoting Section 1999 of the Revised Statutes as proof of the meaning of the Fourteenth Amendment, Judge Dundy said:

Whereas the right of expatriation is a natural and inherent right of all people, indispensable to the enjoyment of the rights of life, liberty and the pursuit of happiness . . . Therefore, any declaration, instruction, opinion, order or decision of any officer of the United States which denies, restricts, impairs, or questions the right of expatriation, is declared inconsistent with the fundamental principles of the republic.[23]

He concluded with this finding: "I think the individual Indian possesses the clear and God-given right to withdraw from his tribe and forever live away from it as though it had no further existence. If the right of expatriation was open to doubt in this country down to the year 1868, certainly since that time no sort of question as to the right can now exist."[24]

*Issue Three: Does the Government Have Authority to Force Removal*

In the last portion of his decision, Judge Dundy said, "I have searched in vain for the semblance of any authority justifying the Commissioner in attempting to remove by force any Indians to any place or any other purpose than what has been stated."[25]

Judge Dundy did not deny the authority of the government in these matters as a general principle, but he said that he was going to weigh its actions against the strict confines of the applicable statutes. He proceeded to quote Section 2149 of the Revised Statutes that gave authority to the commissioner of Indian affairs, with prior consent of the secretary of the interior, "to remove from any tribal reservation any person being thereon without authority of law, or whose presence may be detrimental to the peace and welfare of the Indians."[26] *Note*: The government's interpretation of this statute was that Indians should not be allowed to move from one tribal reservation to another without prior permission of the governing agency, because otherwise the controls imbedded in the reservation system would be in jeopardy.

The judge queried as to where the commissioner was "to look for the necessary force" to carry out his order of removal? Referencing Section 2150 of the Revised Statutes, Judge Dundy stated that "the military arm of the government is the most natural and most potent force to be used on such occasions."[27]

After Judge Dundy presented this statutory background to the question, he recited the fact that: "The relators were found upon the Omaha Indian reservation . . . without lawful authority, and if the Commissioner of Indian Affairs deemed their presence detrimental to the peace and welfare of the Omaha Indians, he had lawful warrant to remove them from the reservation and to employ the necessary military force to effect this object in safety."[28]

Now the question for Judge Dundy became whether General Crook was the proper choice of the government to carry out this removal order? The judge responded in the affirmative, but added that "when the troops are thus employed, they must exercise the authority in the manner provided by Section 2150." This statute required Crook to transport the Relators to the nearest city (Omaha) and "turn them over to the Marshall and U.S. Attorney to be proceeded against in due course of law."[29]

Even though General Crook did not act in strict accordance with Section 2150, Judge Dundy declared "no fault can be imputed to him. He was simply obeying the orders of his superior officers, but the orders as we think, lack the necessary authority of law, and are therefore not binding on the Relators."[30]

The judge's reasoning was based upon his belief that the Ponca Indians were not at war with the government, were not violating any treaty their tribe had entered into, and were not disturbing the peace and welfare of the Omaha tribe since that tribe had invited them to stay with them. Therefore, if they wanted to separate themselves from their own tribe, the judge declared the government "could not lawfully force them back to Indian Territory, to remain and die in that country, against their will . . . I must conclude that no such arbitrary authority exists."[31]

### Ruling

Judge Elmer S. Dundy rendered his landmark ruling, saying "The reasoning advanced in support of my views, leads me to conclude":

1st. That an *Indian* is a PERSON within the meaning of the laws of the United States, and has, therefore, the right to sue out a writ of *habeas corpus* in a federal court, or before a federal judge, in all cases where he may be confined or in custody under color of authority of the United States, or where he is restrained of liberty in violation of the constitution or laws of the United States.

2nd. That General George Crook, the respondent, being commander of the military department of the Platte, has the custody of the relators, under color of authority of the United States, and in violation of the laws thereof.

3rd. That no rightful authority exists for removing by force any of the relators to the Indian Territory, as the respondent has been directed to do.

4th. That the Indians possess the inherent right of expatriation, as well as the more fortunate white race, and have the inalienable right to "*life, liberty*, and the pursuit of happiness," so long as they obey the laws and do not trespass on forbidden ground. And,

5th. Being restrained of liberty under color of authority of the United States, and in violation of the laws thereof, the relators must be discharged from custody, and it is so ordered.[32]

ORDERED ACCORDINGLY.

Fig. 16. (*above*) Judge Elmer S. Dundy.
Courtesy History Nebraska, RG2411-1421-1.

Fig. 17. The *Omaha Daily Herald*,
May 13, 1879.

## STANDING BEARS VICTORY.

Judge Dundy Issues an Order Releasing the Ponca Indians.

A Decision Far Reaching in its Effects.

There is no Law for Using the Military to Force Indians from one Place to Another.

The Indian Ring is Shorn of its Power.

An Indian has Some Rights Which the Courts will Protect.

### SYLLABUS.

United States ex rel. Standing Bear vs. George Crook, a Brigadier General of the Army of the U. S. Before Elmer S. Dundy, U. S. District Judge for Nebraska. Habeas Corpus.

An Indian is a *person* within the meaning of the habeas corpus act, and as such is entitled to sue out a writ of Habeas corpus in the federal court, when it is shown that the petitioner is deprived of liberty under color of authority of the United States, or is in custody of an officer in violation of the constitution, or a law of the United States, or in violation of a treaty made in pursuance thereof.

The right of expatriation is a natural, inherent, and inalianable right, and extends to the Indian as well as to the more fortunate white race.

The commissioner of Indian affairs has ample authority for removing from an Indian reservation all persons found thereon without authority of law, or whose presence may be detrimental to the peace and welfare of the Indians.

The military power of the government may be employed to effect such removal. But where the removal is effected, it is the duty of the troops to convey the persons so removed by the most convenient and safe route, to the civil authorities of the judicial district in which the offence may be committed, to be proceeded against in due course of law.

In time of peace no authority, civil or military, exist for transporting Indians from one section of the country to another without the consent of the Indians, nor to confine them to any particular reservation against their will, and where officers of the government attempt to do this, and arrest and hold Indians who are at peace with the government for the purpose of removing them to, and confining them on, a reservation in the Indian Territory, they will be released on habeas corpus.

A. J. POPPLETON
and
JON. L. WEBSTER,
For the Relators.
G. M. LAMBERTSON
U. S. Attorney for the Government.

# 18

## Standing Bear Keeps His Promise

After the decision had been rendered by Judge Dundy, Standing Bear and the other twenty-nine Poncas were free. They would not be forced to return to Indian Territory. In the meantime, they needed to find a place to live and the means to support themselves. But Standing Bear had something more important on his mind.

### First Attempt to Bury Bear Shield

Standing Bear and his Ponca companions would face arrest if they stepped foot on any other tribe's land, including their ancestral homeland now in the possession of the Lakota Sioux. Webster and Poppleton warned them not to go onto any reservation land. Evidently, a representative of the government contradicted his lawyers and told him it was alright to go onto his old homeland.[1]

Sometime during the evening hours of May 13, 1879, the day following the decision, Standing Bear slipped out of Fort Omaha by himself to go back to his old homeland to bury the bones of his son, as he had promised. He may have been afraid or confused by these two contradictory statements. A soldier notified General Crook that Standing Bear had disappeared. Crook immediately informed Tibbles who guessed where Standing Bear was headed. So Tibbles went in his own buggy to the Omaha reservation. That tribe loaned Tibbles a horse and the services of a "young Indian." They traveled 120 miles in eighteen hours until they finally caught up with Standing Bear on the banks of the Niobrara River. They convinced him to return to Fort Omaha before he was arrested because Crook had not yet received the official order from his military superiors to release the Poncas. Standing Bear returned with Tibbles to Fort Omaha with the bones of Bear Shield in a sack around his neck–unburied.[2]

### The Government's Appeal Is Dismissed

A few days after the court issued its decision, the government filed an appeal in the United States Circuit Court for the District of Nebraska. The May 15,

1879, edition of the *Omaha Herald* reprinted a story from Washington DC concerning a statement by E. A. Hayt, commissioner for Indian Affairs, made the previous day:

> The decision of Judge Dundy at Omaha in the Standing Bear habeas corpus case in which he virtually declares Indians citizens with the right to go where they please, regardless of treaty stipulations is regarded by the government as a heavy blow to the present Indian system, that if sustained will prove extremely dangerous alike to whites and Indians. If the power of the government to hold Indians upon their reservations and to return them when they escape is denied, the Indians will become a body of tramps moving without restraint wherever they please and exposed to attacks of frontiersmen without redress from the government. The district attorney at Omaha has been instructed to take the necessary steps to carry the question to higher courts.[3]

Something extraordinary occurred six months after commissioner Hayt's statement. In January 1880, the U.S. district attorney filed a motion to dismiss the case before the court could even rule on its appeal. Webster and Poppleton gave a report to the Omaha Ponca Indian Committee on July 13, 1880, in which they explained what happened: "The U.S. District Attorney took the case to the United States Circuit Court for this District by appeal, and about May 19th, upon hearing before Mr. Justice Miller, Associate Justice of the Supreme Court of the United States, was there continued, and on January 5th, 1880, the appeal was dismissed on the motion of the U.S. District Attorney."[4]

The obvious question arises as to why would the government file an appeal to the Standing Bear decision and then a few months later file a motion to dismiss its own appeal?

The answer to this unusual motion is found in a letter written by Carl Schurz, secretary of the Interior, dated January 17, 1880. His letter was written in response to a question posed to him by journalist Helen Hunt Jackson:

> As I understand the matter, money is being collected for the purpose of engaging counsel to appear for the Poncas in the courts of the United States, partly to represent them in the case of an appeal from Judge

Dundy's habeas corpus decision, and partly to procure a decision for the recovery of their old reservation on the Missouri River. I believe that the collection of money for these purposes is useless. An appeal from Judge Dundy's habeas corpus decision can proceed only from the Government, not from the Poncas, for the simple reason that the decision was in favor of the latter. An appeal was, indeed, entered by the U. S. District-Attorney at Omaha immediately after the decision had been announced.[5]

Schurz went on in his letter to Jackson to describe how he examined the brief filed in the appeal by the government and made the decision to drop the appeal:

On examining it, I concluded at once to advise the attorney-general of my opinion that it should be dropped, as I could not approve the principles upon which the argument was based. The attorney-general consented to instruct the district-attorney accordingly, and thus Judge Dundy's decision stands without further question on the part of the Government. Had an appeal been prosecuted and had Judge Dundy's decision been sustained by the court above, the general principles involved in it would simply have been affirmed without any other practical effect than that already obtained. This matter is therefore ended.[6]

### Omaha Public Called to Donate

The generosity of the Omaha residents helped the Poncas prepare for their new life. They donated food, money, and other supplies. The May 17, 1879, edition of the *Omaha Daily Herald* reported on the campaign for donations:

Joseph LaFlesche (Iron Eye), the leading man among the Omahas, is in the city. It is proposed to donate provisions to supply them while on the journey. There are several sick in the band and he ought to have a little money for use on the way. Mr. L. S. Reed, on Fourteenth Street between Farnam and Douglas, will receive donations of food or money to be applied for this purpose. There are thirty persons in the party, many of them orphan children, whose parents died in the Indian Territory, and whom he is caring for as a matter of charity. No other case will ever appeal to the sympathy of an ever-generous Omaha public more strongly than this. Send around your donations to Mr. Reed and let us repair in some slight degree the great wrong done to Standing Bear.[7]

### Crook Releases the Poncas

On Monday, May 19, 1879, General Crook received the order from Secretary of War McCray to release the Poncas. That morning the soldiers loaded Standing Bear and his companions onto wagons and escorted them north to the largest of the islands in the Missouri River. This land was considered by the Poncas to be a part of their traditional ancestral homeland. It was located just a few miles from the town of Niobrara, Nebraska. The island was handpicked by Crook because it was outside the boundaries of the Omaha Tribe and the Lakota Sioux, and yet on Ponca home ground. Somehow, this island had not been included in the grant to the Sioux in the 1868 Fort Laramie Treaty. As soon as Standing Bear arrived on the island, he put his people to work chopping trees, building their new homes, and preparing the soil for planting. The people of Niobrara welcomed their return and helped them get settled.[8]

### Bear Shield Is Buried

Finally, Standing Bear and his wife could bury Bear Shield. The traditional Ponca burial grounds were located on the bluffs near the Missouri River.[9] Joe Starita, in *I Am a Man*, described what happened a few months later when Standing Bear and family carried the bones of Bear Shield to his final resting place: "Honoring him with the full ceremonies of the tribe, the father laid Bear Shield's bones to rest, and said good-bye to his son."[10]

The journey Standing Bear and his wife had begun that cold snowy day in January 1879, with the simple purpose of taking the bones of Bear Shield home to be buried among his ancestors, was now completed.

**Standing Bear had kept his promise.**

# 19

## Standing Bear's Gratitude and Generosity

On Sunday, May 18, 1879, the day before the Ponca prisoners were scheduled to be released, Thomas Tibbles rode out to Fort Omaha to say goodbye to Standing Bear. Standing Bear took him and an interpreter to a small hill on the western edge of the fort so he could speak in private.[1] Tibbles did not identify the interpreter; however, if Bright Eyes was still in Omaha from the day Judge Dundy issued his decision, then she likely was the interpreter.

Standing Bear had something pressing upon his mind and heart. He knew he and his people were going to be released shortly, so he had to act swiftly. He wanted to make a gift from his few possessions in gratitude to each of the three men whom he believed helped win his freedom: Thomas H. Tibbles, John L. Webster, and Andrew J. Poppleton.

### Gift to Thomas Tibbles—"You Are My Brother"

Standing Bear took Tibbles and the interpreter to the tent where he had been imprisoned for nearly two months and opened his trunk. He presented Tibbles with his beaded buckskin leggings. Standing Bear was tremendously grateful to Tibbles for all he had done over the past six weeks to assemble the legal team, to publicize his story nationally, to stir up support within the Omaha community, and to relay his request to Judge Dundy to grant him the opportunity to speak for himself in court. Standing Bear said to Tibbles:

> I remember the dark day when you first came to speak to me. I know if it had not been for what you have done for me I would now be a prisoner in the Indian Territory, and many of these who are with me here would have been in their graves . . . While there is one Ponca alive you will never be without a friend. Mr. Poppleton and Mr. Webster are my friends. You are my brother.[2]

After making his gift to Tibbles, Standing Bear expressed a desire to visit his two lawyers that Sunday afternoon. He wanted to say goodbye, and to present each with a gift in gratitude for their services to him and his people.[3]

### *Gift to John Webster—"I Can Now Seek the Ways of Peace"*

Tibbles drove Standing Bear and the interpreter in his horse and buggy to the home of John L. Webster. Upon entering Webster's home, Tibbles reported that Standing Bear "shook hands with all present remarking that he wished to pay respect to the ladies and he would shake hands with them first."[4] Before making his gift to Webster, Standing Bear made a brief speech:

> You and I are here. Our skins are of a different color, but God made us both. A little while ago when I was young, I was wild. I knew nothing of the ways of the white people. I see you have a nice house here. I look at these beautiful rooms. I would like to have a house too, and it may be after a while that I can get one, but not so good a house as this. That is what I want to do. For a great many years, a hundred years or more, the white men have been driving us about. They are shrewd, sharp and know how to cheat. But since I have been here, I have found them different. They have all treated me very kindly. I am very thankful for it.[5]

Then with his tomahawk in hand, Standing Bear made a formal presentation of his symbolic gift to Webster, saying:

> Hitherto when we have been wronged, we went to war. To assert our rights and avenge our wrongs we took the tomahawk. We had no law to punish those who did wrong, so we took our tomahawks and went to kill. . . . But you have found a better way. You have gone into the court for us and I find our wrongs can be righted there. Now I have no more use for the tomahawk. I want to lay it down forever. [at this point he stooped down, laid the tomahawk on the floor, and then stood erect and folded his arms and said:] I lay it down. I have no more use for it. I have found a better way. [then picking it up he handed it to Mr. Webster and said:] I present it to you as a token of my gratitude, that you may keep it in remembrance of this great victory you have gained. I have no further use for it. I can now seek the ways of peace.[6]

Webster thanked Standing Bear for his gift saying it was "a duty to humanity and to God to extend to your people the benefit and protection of our laws."[7] Webster finished his remarks by confirming his personal commitment to help ensure that the American legal system functioned for the benefit of Standing Bear and his people: "I shall continue to fight your battles as long as it is necessary to give you the protection of the laws, and I rejoice to know that you have come to believe the tomahawk is of no further service to you."[8]

### Gift to Andrew Poppleton—"God Sent You to Help Me"

Leaving John Webster's home, Tibbles drove Standing Bear and the interpreter to the home of Andrew J. Poppleton. Standing Bear greeted Mr. Poppleton and his wife Caroline, and made a presentation of his most valued possession, his ancestral headdress, telling his lawyer:

> I believe I told you in the court room, that God made me and that I was a man. For many years, we have been chased about, as a dog chases a wild beast. God sent you to help me. I thank you for what you have done. I want to get my land back. That is what I long for all the time. I wish to live there and be buried with my fathers. When you were speaking in the court room, of course I could not understand, but I could see that you were trying very hard to release me. I think you are doing for me and my people, something that never has been done before. If I had to pay you for it, I could never get enough to do it. I have here a relic which has come down to my people, through a great many generations. I do not know how old it is. It may be two or three hundred years old. I desire to present it to you for what you have done for me.[9]

Upon receiving the gift, Tibbles reported, Poppleton told Standing Bear that he was satisfied he had done something to help him and the Poncas "secure their rights."[10]

In 1915 Caroline Poppleton wrote an article, "The War Bonnet," in which she shared her thoughts and feelings of that memorable afternoon in her home. Thirty-six years later she was still touched by his eloquence and generosity, saying:

> I remember in 1879 how Standing Bear with his interpreter called upon Mr. Poppleton at his rooms on the corner of Harney and Fifteenth where we boarded after our house on Capitol Hill was burned, to personally thank him for his speech on his behalf and with the War Bonnet in his hands, he offered it to Mr. Poppleton as his grateful act and his only pay

for the words he had spoke for him and his tribe. . . . Out of the poverty of his worldly possessions, he gave such visible token of his appreciation as he could, while *out of the wealth of his human soul, and out of the fullness of his manly heart*, he uttered sentiments, and expressed purposes which distinguish him as chief among ten thousand, and as a character, dark though his skin may be, altogether lovely.[11]

### Summary

Standing Bear, in his kind and gracious manner, made gifts from his meager but treasured personal possessions to the three men who helped him the most to become a free man. To Thomas Tibbles, he gave his beaded buckskin leggings and called him his brother. To John Webster, he gave his tomahawk and said he had no further need of it. To Andrew Poppleton, he gave his prized headdress and said he was grateful God had sent Poppleton to help him.

Standing Bear's spirit of gratitude extended to many around him. He told Tibbles that same day that he was especially grateful on behalf of his fellow Ponca prisoners for "the kind treatment they have received from the soldiers, and the medicine which the army doctor has given them, which has saved their lives."[12]

**The spirit of Standing Bear's quest for freedom would soon spread across the nation and kindle a fire for justice and reform.**

# 20

## A Fire Kindled

As soon as the decision was issued by Judge Dundy, the government stopped all provisions for Standing Bear and his companions. The government felt it was no longer under any treaty obligation to provide food, supplies, seed, or tools to individual Poncas who had legally separated from their tribe. However, out of this bad situation a positive response was mobilized.

### Omaha Ponca Relief Committee

Thomas Tibbles and Episcopal bishop Robert H. Clarkson rallied clergy and community support for these newly freed Poncas by creating the Omaha Ponca Relief Committee. The chair of the committee was Bishop Clarkson. Members included Rev. A. F. Sherrill, pastor of a Congregational church, Rev. W. J. Harsha, pastor of a Presbyterian church, Leavitt Burnham, W. M. Yates, and P. L. Perine.[1]

The committee helped the Poncas get settled in their new home with food, clothing, plows, pitchforks, lumber wagons, tools, and seed. In addition, the committee secured funds for future legal battles to be waged on behalf of the Ponca cause, and to support Tibbles as he and others went east to galvanize public opinion for Indian reform.

### Bright Eyes and Iron Eye Go to Indian Territory

Tibbles reported that after a discussion with General Crook, John Webster, and others, the committee sent Chief Iron Eye and Bright Eyes to Indian Territory to visit her sick aunt and uncle, and to inform them of Judge Dundy's decision.[2] In her testimony before the Senate Select Committee on February 13, 1880, Bright Eyes said she traveled to Indian Territory "in the latter part of May with my father," because "we received word that my aunt was very sick."[3] After meeting with her aunt and uncle, they asked permission to bring them home to the Omaha reservation, "but the Agent refused."[4] Some of the people told her that agent William Whiteman "was a very domineering sort of a man; and if the Indians did not obey, he would take measures to see that they did."[5]

In the short time Bright Eyes and Iron Eye were in Indian Territory, they found the 550 Poncas living in tents and shanties, with no stoves or bed stands; despite the fact that the agency house had been beautifully built and furnished. She said "the Indians had told me they wanted to work for themselves, but they had no horses."[6] Some of the women told her they wanted a few wagons to haul things, but the agent refused "because he was afraid they would run away with them."[7] Bright Eyes noticed how sickly the Poncas were, so one day she spoke with a physician who told her, "I really believe that what made the Poncas sick is the water. Some of them cannot drink it without vomiting it right up."[8]

Bright Eyes also met with Chief White Eagle, who asked her to write a letter for him addressed to the people of the United States, describing the condition of the tribe living in Indian Territory. White Eagle told her "they had heard of Mr. Tibbles, and what he had done for Standing Bear; and they wanted to see whether something could not be done for them."[9] Bright Eyes said these Poncas wanted to take their annuity money owed them by the government and apply it to a lawsuit on their behalf; but White Eagle told her, "We are too poor."[10] In early June, Bright Eyes and Iron Eye returned to Nebraska after spending only a week in Indian Territory.

### Tibbles Travels East

Tibbles, Webster, Bishop Clarkson, and the members of the Omaha Ponca Relief Committee started a campaign to raise public awareness of the plight of the Poncas, the importance of the court decision, and the need to raise funds to continue more legal battles. They sent Tibbles east to start this campaign.

Tibbles resigned as deputy editor of the *Omaha Daily Herald* and left for Chicago in late June 1879. Chicago was likely selected as the first city to visit because of a favorable article in the May 16, 1879, edition of the *Chicago Tribune*, which stated: "Out in Omaha at least, the idea has come to the surface at last, that an Indian is a man with human rights, and not a mere head of livestock to be shipped from place to place and imprisoned at the whim of military officers, or starved to death by agents who will profit by the starving. . . . All honor to Tibbles! But now what is to become of the Poncas."[11]

When Tibbles arrived in Chicago, he met with some reporters and shared the Ponca story with them. He spoke at public gatherings and was successful in raising money, which he sent back to the treasurer of the Omaha Ponca Relief Committee.[12]

Moving on to Boston, he met with Edward Everett Hale, who wrote a supporting editorial in the *Boston Advertiser*. Tibbles spoke at a large public gathering and received encouragement and support of community leaders, including abolitionist Wendell Phillips. He arrived back in Omaha on September 6, 1879.[13]

### Bright Eyes' First Public Speech

Tibbles returned to Omaha just in time to attend a lecture by Standing Bear and Bright Eyes at Rev. William J. Harsha's Presbyterian church. In a brief but highly emotional speech, Bright Eyes nearly fainted as she concluded with the story of the death of her cousin Prairie Flower occurring on the forced march to Indian Territory in 1877, and her subsequent burial by some Christian women in Milford, Nebraska.

The reaction to her speech, as well as the success of Tibbles trip to Chicago and Boston, convinced the leaders of the Omaha Ponca Relief Committee to send Tibbles, Standing Bear, Bright Eyes, and her nineteen-year-old brother, Francis LaFlesche (Woodworker) to the East Coast, to promote the Ponca cause in a series of lectures before public audiences. The four boarded a train in mid-October 1879.

### East Coast Lecture Tour

For the first time, citizens in Pittsburgh, Boston, New York, Philadelphia, and Washington DC, listened to Standing Bear and Bright Eyes tell their story with eloquence and passion. The response they received gave them hope that the Poncas, and all Native Americans, would no longer be invisible in the minds and hearts of the public.

One evening in late October 1879, the manager of the Boston hotel where the group was staying gave Tibbles a telegram informing him that his wife, Amelia Owens Tibbles, had suddenly died of peritonitis back in Omaha. He went to his room and cried. Soon Standing Bear came into his room and started praying and comforting the man he called "my brother." They were joined by Francis LaFlesche who showed Tibbles a telegram Standing Bear had just received, informing him that his brother Big Snake was dead at the hands of government soldiers. The two friends comforted each other in a time of mutual grief and agreed to stay the course and not abandon the tour.[14] Worried about who was taking care of his two daughters, Eda and May, who were nine and eleven years old, Webster sent Tibbles another telegram saying he had placed them in a private school and some good people in Omaha would look after them until he could return home.[15]

The group of four achieved its greatest notoriety in Boston, where Francis Prucha reported, "Prominent men organized the Boston Indian Citizenship Committee to fight for the rights of the Poncas and other Indians."[16] On December 2, 1879, the group lectured at a noontime gathering in Faneuil Hall. It was reported that Bright Eyes was the first woman to ever give a public speech in that historic venue.[17]

At one of the events in Boston, Tibbles was approached by a young ethnologist, Alice C. Fletcher, who expressed a desire to observe firsthand how Native Americans lived and worked. Two years later she arrived in Omaha. Tibbles and Bright Eyes took her on a tour of the Omaha village, and then introduced her to Standing Bear and the Poncas.[18] For the next twenty years, Fletcher studied their culture and then in 1911 published *The Omaha Tribe*, with her fellow researcher Francis LaFlesche.

In February 1880 the four spoke before large public gatherings in Philadelphia, then traveled to Washington DC where Tibbles, Standing Bear, and Bright Eyes testified before the Senate Select Committee. In May 1880 they returned to Omaha. The tour was deemed a great success.

Newspaper reporters and editors, members of the clergy, and influential citizens took up the cause for Indian reform, including Delano A. Goddard, editor of the *Boston Daily Advertiser*, Whitelaw Reid, editor of the *New York Daily Tribune*, Massachusetts senator Henry L. Dawes, poet Henry Wadsworth Longfellow, ethnologist Alice C. Fletcher, publisher Henry Houghton, and muckraking journalist Helen Hunt Jackson.

### Helen Hunt Jackson's Crusade

Helen Hunt Jackson attended one of their talks in Boston. She was so energized that she put all her efforts for the next six years into researching the story of the government's neglect of the Poncas and other Native American tribes. Her work, *A Century of Dishonor*, included hundreds of letters to congressmen, newspaper editors, and government officials.

During the East Coast tour, Thomas Tibbles's book, *The Ponca Chiefs* (1881), was published. Abolitionist Wendell Phillips wrote the dedication: "To the people of the United States this narrative is respectfully dedicated as

Fig. 18. Susette LaFlesche Tibbles (Bright Eyes). Courtesy History Nebraska, RG2026-05.

a fair specimen of the system of injustice, oppression and robbery which the government calls 'its Indian policy.'"[19] Bright Eyes wrote the introduction to the book, saying, "It is a little thing, a simple thing, which my people ask of a nation whose watchword is liberty; but it is endless in its consequences. They ask for their liberty, and *law is liberty*" (emphasis in original).[20]

Helen Hunt Jackson asked Tibbles the origin of Bright Eyes's phrase, "law is liberty." Tibbles replied saying that one evening he observed Bright Eyes looking out a window gazing upon men and women walking in all directions as they pleased. Bright Eyes said to Tibbles, "That is being free; it is because they have law to take care of them that they can go."[21]

Bright Eyes had developed a deep personal relationship with Helen Hunt Jackson, so when Tibbles received the news Jackson had died in August 1885, he said Bright Eyes cried and mourned the loss of her great friend.[22]

There may have been no one more affected or stirred to action by Standing Bear and Judge Dundy's decision during the East Coast lecture tour than Helen Hunt Jackson. It became a crusade for her. In a letter to Charles Dudley Warner, editor of the *Hartford Daily Courant*, dated December 21, 1879, she wrote: "I shall be found with 'Indians' engraved on my brain when I am dead. *A fire has been kindled within me, which will never go out*" (emphasis added).[23]

# 21

## Redress for Wrongs

The federal government initiated two historic investigations in 1880 to determine the facts surrounding the forced removal of the Ponca Tribe to Indian Territory, and to discuss possible redress for wrongs committed to the Poncas.

### Congressional Investigation

The U.S. Senate appointed a select committee in 1880 to investigate the "Removal of the Ponca Indians." The committee was chaired by Senator Henry Dawes of Massachusetts, who had heard Tibbles, Bright Eyes, and Standing Bear speak in Boston.[1]

In February 1880 Standing Bear, Bright Eyes, and Thomas Tibbles met with the committee in Washington DC to give their personal testimonies. Chief White Eagle, Edward Kemble, and others were also called to testify in the ensuing days.

The committee's report of May 31, 1880, concluded that the Poncas were forced to Indian Territory without legal authority and a great wrong was done to them:

> In all accounts of the character of these Indians, and in all mention of them in official reports, they are described as among the most peaceful and quiet of all the Indians in the United States. Their disposition toward the United States has been uniformly friendly; they had never been known to cause trouble or disturbance, to make war upon the Indians, or upon settlers. They were always ready, and on many occasions did render us valuable assistance.

The report recommended that the wrong done to the Poncas should be quickly redressed by the government:

> If the government expects to exterminate this tribe, it has but to continue the policy of the past few years. The committee can see no valid

objection, therefore, to that means of redress which comes nearest to putting these Indians in precisely the condition they were in when E.C. Kemble undertook, without authority of law, to force them from their homes into the Indian Territory ... This proceeding on the part of the United States was without justification and was a great wrong to this peaceable tribe of Indians and demands at the hands of the United States speedy and full redress.[2]

### Presidential Investigation

The Ponca Commission was created by President Rutherford B. Hayes on December 18, 1880, to investigate the removal of the Ponca Tribe to Indian Territory. He appointed Brig. Gen. George Crook to serve as chairman. The other committee members were Brig. Gen. Nelson A. Miles, William Stickney (secretary of the Board of Indian Commissioners), and Walter Allen (Boston Indian Citizenship Committee). General Crook named Lt. John G. Bourke as the commission's secretary.

President Hayes directed the commission members "to ascertain the facts in regard to their [the Ponca Tribe] removal and present condition, so far as was necessary to determine the question as to what justice and humanity require should be done by the Government of the United States."[3]

The members of the commission first traveled to Indian Territory to take testimony from Chief White Eagle and other Poncas. They then traveled to Niobrara, Nebraska, to meet with Standing Bear and his companions.[4]

Lieutenant Bourke wrote in his diary that when the commission members and staff arrived in the Ponca village on January 11, 1881, the weather was bitter:

The thermometer indicated 14 degrees. Snow lay to a great depth, in level places 12–14 inches, in drifts of at least 5ft. Crossing the Niobrara River to a large island, we reached the village of the Poncas-consisting of both tipis and log-houses. Chief Standing Bear and his brother, Yellow Horse, and the old chief Smoke Maker and several others came up to shake hands. ... The Poncas have ponies, wagons, cattle, hogs, hay and wood piles and other indications of thrift and increasing comfort. A supply of blankets had just reached them from friends in Omaha, Nebraska which they were engaged in distributing among their women and children. This year, they have cultivated over 100 acres of corn, which is stored in granaries and have been, with the exception of some little assistance from sympathizing friends in Boston and Omaha, independent of outside help.[5]

Bourke reported that Rev. James Dorsey and David LeClair were present as interpreters. General Crook began the meeting by asking Dorsey "to explain to them that we come here by order of the President, to find out their situation; and we want them to answer all questions as put to them unreservedly. They can rest assured that we are their friends and they can speak freely."[6]

### Ponca Commissioners Hear Standing Bear's Testimony

Standing Bear began by saying, "I do not think that we have made this day, but I think that God has caused it, and my heart is glad to see you all here."[7] He described the sadness felt at the loss of their property at the time of the 1877 removal: "Your land is your own and so are your things, and you wouldn't like anybody to come and try to take them away from you. If men want to trade they say 'how much do you want for that piece of property? What price do you put upon it?' But nothing of that kind was said. They came and took me away without saying a word."[8]

General Miles asked Standing Bear what property was taken from him and its value. Standing Bear replied:

I will tell you what I had: you will know how much it was worth. I made a house for myself; I cut the logs and built it myself. I built a stable and pen for my hogs: I built them myself: I bought a stove for $30. I had tools and farming implements, plows, harrows, pitchforks, spades, shovels—all those things. I had two beds and a closet full of dishes, and a table. I had two lamps. I had a cat and I left her and she was in a pitiful condition. I had two cows, three hogs. I am not the only one who had these things, but we all had such things . . . We all left the same things; the property of the tribe was left behind in the house.[9]

Standing Bear paused to express his gratitude to some of the commission members for aid they had given him:

I have come back to my own land and I think that two of the Commissioners (pointing to Generals Crook and Miles) have had something
to do with this. I was brought up before the Court and it released me.
This, I think is one of my principal friends from Boston (pointing to Mr.
Allen): one of those who have been my friends, by day and by night:
one of those who have been trying to raise me out of the darkness. My
friends, whatever I tell you to-day, I hope that you will carry back to the
Great Father and give him an exact account of it. I hope you will tell him
that I am living on my old land and that I am doing well there and that
I am working for myself.[10]

Finally, Standing Bear responded to questions as to what type and amount
of compensation he and the Poncas with him, as well as those remaining
in Indian Territory, should receive from the government, saying: "I do not
wish to go elsewhere. . . . Whatever damages are coming to us, and whatever annuities, I want them to be split in two, one part for us Poncas here,
and one part for the Poncas in Indian Territory. I desire you to help me in
this. I don't want an agent. I want to have a teacher or a minister. I want a
missionary to be with me, and to attend to me."[11]

### Ponca Commission Report Issued (1881)

The *Report of the Ponca Commission* was certified on January 25, 1881, by
Lieutenant Bourke and presented to President Hayes at the White House
by the commission members the next day. The commission discovered
that the Ponca removal to Indian Territory was illegal, causing them unjust
hardship, but that through hard work they had become self-sufficient. The
report made the following conclusions:

That the lands from which the Poncas were removed had been ceded
and relinquished to them by the United States for ample consideration
specified in the treaties. That the government solemnly covenanted not
only to warrant and defend their title to these lands, but also to protect
their persons and property thereon.

That the Indians had violated no condition of the treaty by which their
title to the lands or claims to protection had been forfeited, and that
this rightful claim still exists in full force and effect, notwithstanding

all acts done by the government of the United States. That the Indians who have returned to their reservation in Dakota have the strongest possible attachment to their lands and a resolute purpose to retain them.

That they have received no assistance from the government and except the limited aid furnished by benevolent people, they have been entirely self-sustaining. With few agricultural implements they have cultivated a considerable tract of land for their support. They are on friendly terms with all other Indian Tribes, including the Sioux, as well as with the white settlers in their vicinity. They pray that they may not again be disturbed.[12]

The commission recommended that the Poncas be given land on their former reservation equal to "160 acres to each man, woman and child of the Ponca Tribe", an appropriation of money "for agricultural implements, stock, seed, and construction of comfortable dwellings and a schoolhouse," and that "all Indians should have the opportunity of appealing to the courts for the protection and vindication of their rights of person and property."[13]

### Summary of Actions to Redress Wrongs

Following the recommendations of these two government investigations, Congress made an appropriation of $165,000 on March 3, 1881, to indemnify the Ponca tribe for losses sustained in consequence of the removal, and to declare their right to go back onto their old homeland. The appropriation was to be made as follows:

- ▸ To the Southern Poncas $50,000 to buy 101,000 acres from the Cherokees; $20,000 to buy livestock and as cash stipends.
- ▸ To the Northern Poncas $10,000 cash stipends, $5000 for building, $5000 for education, $5000 for livestock, seed and other farming products.
- ▸ $70,000 to be placed into a trust fund to earn 5% interest to be split among all Poncas equally on an annual basis.[14]

Later in that same year, Interior secretary Samuel J. Kirkwood, who had replaced Carl Schurz, met with representatives of the Lakota Sioux and Ponca Tribes in Washington DC. It was agreed that the Lakota Sioux would cede to the Poncas twenty-six thousand acres of the original ninety-six thousand

Fig. 19. Standing Bear and family on his own allotted land, 1903.
Courtesy History Nebraska, RG 2039-08.

Fig. 20. Standing Bear family beside home and gardens, 1903.
Courtesy History Nebraska, RG 2039-09.

Fig. 21. The Poncas' homeland in Nebraska (1903), showing Standing Bear's allotment (*top right, shaded*) and the allotment of Otto Knudsen (grandfather of Judi gaiashkibos) (*south of Standing Bear's land*). Courtesy of Judi M. gaiashkibos, executive director, Nebraska Commission on Indian Affairs.

acres which the government had through a "clerical error" taken from the Poncas in the Fort Laramie Treaty of 1868.[15]

In 1887 Congress passed the Dawes Severalty Act. It allocated to each Indian head of household up to 320 acres, up to 160 acres for a single adult, up to 160 acres for minors who were orphans, and up to 80 acres for all other minors. Tribal land for centuries had been held in severalty (i.e., by the tribe as a whole). This was an important element of their culture and identity. The Dawes Act led to much consternation among Native Americans and supporters of Indian Reform, because in less than fifty years after its passage two-thirds of the land allocated to individual Native Americans had been lost due to tax foreclosures and forced sales.[16]

The allotment to Standing Bear was nearly three hundred acres located on the west bank of the Niobrara River. There he would build his own home and farm his own land until his death in 1908.

# 22

## The Standing Bear Decision Sets Precedent

In the same year the Senate Select Committee and the Ponca Commission began their investigations into the forced removal of the Poncas to Indian Territory, Webster and Poppleton filed two new lawsuits in federal court before Judge Dundy. One case was filed on behalf of the Ponca Tribe, and the other case was filed on behalf of John Elk, a Winnebago. The Elk case went all the way to the United States Supreme Court.

### Ponca Tribe Lawsuit (1880)

The Ponca Tribe sought a ruling from the court confirming title to land ceded to them by the government in the Treaty of 1865. On April 3, 1880, Webster and Poppleton filed *Ponca Tribe of Indians* (plaintiff) *v. Makh-pi-ah-lu-tah, or Red Cloud, in his own behalf and in behalf of the Sioux Tribe of Indians* (defendant) in the United States District Court for the District of Nebraska, in front of Judge Dundy.

The December 4, 1880, edition of the *Omaha Daily Bee* summarized the issue: "The Plaintiffs claim that if the Poncas acquired a title in fee simple, they had and still have a vested right in the lands, which cannot be divested by Congress without their consent and upon adequate consideration."[1]

Judge Dundy ruled in favor of the Ponca Tribe. His decision issued on December 3, 1880, declared: "the Ponca Tribe of Indians, Plaintiff, has a legal estate in and is entitled to the possession of the real property described in the Petition, and that the Sioux Nation of Indians, unlawfully keeps the Ponca Tribe of Indians out of the possession of the same."[2]

### Elk v. Wilkins *Lawsuit (1880)*

The second important case filed by Webster and Poppleton in 1880 involved John Elk, a Winnebago. Elk had severed his relations with his tribe and lived with a white family in Omaha. On April 5, 1880, he tried to register to vote in the upcoming city election. Charles Wilkins, registrar for the Fifth Ward, refused to allow him to register since he was not a citizen. Nebraska had not passed legislation granting citizenship to Native Americans.

Webster and Poppleton filed *Elk v. Wilkins* in the federal circuit court in Omaha. The case was heard before circuit court judges Dundy and George McCrary. The defendant, Charles Wilkins, was represented by federal district attorney Lambertson. The same three lawyers involved in the Standing Bear case were back in Judge Dundy's courtroom once again.

District Attorney Genio M. Lambertson filed a demurrer citing the plaintiff's failure to state a proper cause of action because only citizens could vote in a Nebraska election, and therefore, in his opinion, the court was without jurisdiction to hear this matter. The two judges concurred and dismissed the case. Webster and Poppleton filed an appeal to the United States Supreme Court.[3]

In 1884 the United States Supreme Court affirmed the lower court's decision against John Elk, ruling: "The State of Nebraska is not shown to have taken any action affecting the condition of the plaintiff. The Plaintiff, not being a citizen of the United States under the 14th Amendment of the constitution, has been deprived of no right secured by the 15th Amendment, and cannot maintain this action."[4]

Even though John Elk lost his case and plea for citizenship, the *Elk v. Wilkins* case is important because it is evident that the Standing Bear decision emboldened Elk, Webster, and Poppleton to file suit in federal court to test the issue of citizenship. The case proved that an individual Native American who had severed ties with his tribe could have his day in court, seeking redress of his grievances. Within five years of the Standing Bear decision, a Native American had his case heard before the U.S. Supreme Court.[5] Citizenship would finally be granted to Native Americans by Congress in 1924.

### Standing Bear Decision Cited as Authority

Since 1879 the decision rendered by Judge Dundy in the Standing Bear case has been cited in courts throughout the United States as authority for two important issues: the definition of "person," and the right of expatriation.[6]

**Authority for Definition of Person.** The Standing Bear decision has been cited as authority for the definition of the word "person." "The word "person" as it is ordinarily used means a living human being. It is so defined in Webster's and in Johnson's and in the Century Dictionaries. It is so defined by the courts, U. S. v. Crook, 25 Fed. Case. 695." *State ex* *rel. Bancroft v. Frear, Secretary of State*, Supreme Court of Wisconsin, 128 N.W. 1068 (1910).

**Authority for Right of Expatriation.** The Standing Bear decision has also been cited as authority in determining the nature and scope of evidence a court may require to decide whether a Native American has severed ties with a tribe (the right of expatriation):

> Tribal membership is a bilateral relation, depending for its existence not only upon the action of the Tribe but also the action of the individual concerned. Any member of any Indian tribe is at full liberty to terminate his tribal relationship whenever he so chooses ... A member of an Indian tribe "possesses the clear and God given right to withdraw from his tribe and forever live away from it as though it had not further existence." United States ex. Rel. Standing Bear v. Crook, 25 F. Cas. 695,649 (Circ. Ct. D.Neb.1879). *In the Matter of the Adoption of C.D.K., a Minor Child*, United States District Court of Utah, 2009 WL 2494618 (2009).

In 1941 Felix S. Cohen (1907-53) wrote the *Handbook of Federal Indian Law* in which he compiled all of the various treaties, statutes, and court decisions, including the importance of the Standing Bear case:

> Oppression against a racial minority is more terrible than most other forms of oppression because there is no escape from one's race. There is one federal case which squarely raised the question whether Indians can avoid oppression at the hands of the Federal Government by renouncing their allegiance to their tribe and abandoning the reservation assigned to their use. The case of United States ex.rel. Standing Bear v. Crook aroused out of an attempt of a band of Ponca Indians led by Chief Standing Bear to escape from a reservation in Indian Territory to which they had been removed by the Interior Department.

Cohen discussed the significance of Judge Dundy's decision, concluding that in granting the writ against General Crook "The federal Court established a precedent which many Indians since Standing Bear have followed, and which many administrators since General Crook have recognized. *The right of expatriation established by the Standing Bear case remains a significant human right.*"[7]

## *Summary*

The Standing Bear decision set the precedent for all Native Americans to file petitions in federal court seeking redress for their grievances. As "persons" in the eyes of the law, they now had "standing to sue" in federal court for the first time in American history. The historic decision was the first step in the civil rights journey of Native Americans for equality under the American legal system. The journey would be long. More suffering would be endured, and setbacks would occur.

**But the precedent had been set.**[8]

# 23

## A Nation Aroused from the Sin of Indifference

In her introduction to Thomas Tibbles's *The Ponca Chiefs*, Bright Eyes wrote that the whole nation had been aroused from its "sin of indifference" as a result of the Standing Bear decision:

> It is a little thing, a simple thing, which my people ask of a nation whose watchword is liberty; but it is endless in its consequences. They ask for liberty, and law is liberty. "We did not know of these wrongs," say the magistrates. Is not that only the cry of "Am I my brother's keeper?" For years the petitions of my people have gone up unnoticed, unheeded by all but their Creator, and now at last a man of your race has arisen, who has shown faith enough in humanity to arouse the nation from the sin of indifference.[1]

The words of Bright Eyes reflect the tangible benefits the court's decision had on the nation in the decades that followed: (1) Standing Bear's personal quest to be free was achieved, along with his small group of Poncas; (2) the government's policy of forced removal of tribes ended; (3) a movement for Indian reform was mobilized; (4) citizenship for Native Americans was openly discussed and promoted; (5) access to the federal court system was opened to Native Americans for redress of their grievances; (6) a portion of the ancestral homeland of the Poncas was restored, and financial appropriations were made as compensation for the unjust taking of their land; and (7) local community support groups arose in Omaha, Chicago, and Boston.

### Quest for Freedom Won

The first effect of Judge Dundy's decision was the personal freedom of thirty Ponca men, women, and children. The cloud of uncertainty that hung over their heads for fifty-four days and nights regarding when the soldiers would take them back to Indian Territory was lifted. They no longer had to live in constant fear and worry about going back to sickness and death, but instead could look forward to going home and starting a new life with their families.

There was an additional blessing for Standing Bear and his wife Susette. Bear Shield could finally be buried in his ancestral homeland. Standing Bear's quest for freedom had been achieved. These Poncas could live in peace.

### Forced Removal Policy Ended

After the Standing Bear decision, no other Native American tribe was subjected to a forced removal from their homeland to Indian Territory. The pressure from Eastern newspapers, public forums, and government investigations had been great enough to stop forced removals.

### Movement for Indian Reform Mobilized

Newspaper reporters across the nation, including Thomas Tibbles, made Americans aware of Judge Dundy's ruling. The *Chicago Tribune* stated in its May 13, 1879, edition that it was "the only case of the kind ever brought on behalf of Indians in Federal Court."[2]

Muckraking journalist Helen Hunt Jackson boldly declared, "Will not the name of Judge Dundy stand by the side of that of Abraham Lincoln in the matter of emancipation acts?"[3]

The East Coast lecture tour made by Tibbles, Bright Eyes, Francis LaFlesche, and Standing Bear in 1879–80 mobilized public opinion in support of moving forward with investigations and efforts to redress some of the wrongs committed.

Within seven months of Judge Dundy's decision, the United States Senate created a special select committee to investigate what happened to the Poncas that led to the court's decision. Standing Bear, Thomas Tibbles, and Chief White Eagle all testified before the committee. For the first time in American history, a Native American woman, Susette LaFlesche (Bright Eyes), was called to testify before a congressional committee. In addition, the president of the United States created his own commission to investigate the matter. The report issued by the Ponca Commission called for restoration of land and allocation of money and goods to compensate the Poncas for the wrongs done to them.

### Citizenship Discussed and Promoted

The issue of citizenship for Native Americans was now openly discussed in public forums, newspaper editorials, and in the hallways of Congress, because of Judge Dundy's decision.

Professor James King noted General Crook's continued involvement after the decision was rendered and his interest in the citizenship issue, saying "he maintained his contact with Tibbles and found new allies among Eastern Humanitarians. In the next decade he would become a leader in efforts to bring education and citizenship to the Indian."[4]

Lt. John G. Bourke confirmed Crook's leadership role in this effort by inserting into his diary a letter the general wrote to Tibbles dated June 19, 1879, in which Crook said:

Our Indians act under precisely the same impulses and are guided by identically the same trains of reasoning as would white men under like circumstances . . . But I am very sorry to say, they have, to a very great degree, lost confidence in our people and their promises . . . It seems to me to be an odd feature of our judicial system that the only people in this country who have no rights under the law are the original owners of the soil. . . . The true and only policy to pursue with the Indian is to treat him just as we treat a white man.[5]

In the same year Tibbles published *The Ponca Chiefs*, Rev. William Harsha, pastor of the First Presbyterian Church in Omaha, asked his friend Bright Eyes to write an introduction to his book *Plowed Under: The Story of an Indian Chief*. Bright Eyes wrote under her tribal name Inshta-Theamba: "The white people have tried to solve the *Indian Question* by commencing with the proposition that the Indian is different from all other human beings." She suggested a different solution:

Allow an Indian to suggest that the solution of the vexed "Indian Question" is *Citizenship*, with all its attending duties and responsibilities, as well as the privileges of protection under the law, by which the Indian could appeal to the courts, when deprived of life, liberty or property, as every citizen can, and would be allowed the opportunity to make something of himself in common with every other citizen.[6]

In 1924 Congress passed the Indian Freedom Citizenship Suffrage Act (known as the Snyder Act), named after its sponsor, Rep. Homer P. Snyder (NY):

> Be it enacted by the Senate and House of Representatives of the United
> States of America in Congress assembled, that all non-citizen Indians
> born in the territorial limits of the United States be, and they are hereby,
> declared to be citizens of the United States: Provided, that the granting
> of such citizenship shall not in any manner impair or otherwise affect
> the right of any Indian to tribal or other property.[7]

The last states to grant the franchise to Native Americans were Arizona
and New Mexico in 1948, and Utah in 1962. The Voting Rights Act of 1965
strengthened these state actions.

### Access Granted to Federal Court

The Standing Bear decision opened the door to individual Native Americans to file actions in federal court seeking a redress of their grievances.
*Elk v. Wilkins*, filed by Webster and Poppleton in 1880, confirmed this fact.
As "persons" under the Fourteenth Amendment to the Constitution, they
now had standing to file an action in federal court.

The precedent set by Judge Dundy's decision for Native Americans and
their lawyers, granting the right to turn to the courtroom to resolve issues and
grievances, cannot be overstated. James A. Lake Sr., professor of law, wrote
that the decision was "one of the few praiseworthy episodes in nineteenth
century White-Indian relations, as well as an example of the superiority of
law over force as a solution to human problems."[8]

### Financial Compensation for Land Taken

In addition to the restoration of some of the land taken from the Poncas
and other tribes as earlier discussed, Congress created the Indian Claims
Commission in 1946 and offered each of the dispossessed tribes five years
to organize and lodge their formal claims for compensation of land taken
from them. Professor David Wishart noted the Poncas were awarded compensation in 1972 for their following claims:

> *Docket 322* involved the 1858 cession of Ponca land. They "were awarded
> $1,878,500 representing the difference between what they were orig-
> inally paid (19.5 cents per acre) and what they should have been paid
> ($1.00 per acre)."[9]

*Docket 323* involved the 1877 removal of the Poncas to Indian Territory. They "were granted the difference between the consideration and the fair market value of the land ($174,327), but allotted 5% interest a year on the principal, because the taking had been without consent. By the time of the final judgment in 1972, the award had accumulated to $1,013,425."[10]

## Community Zeal Ignited

One of the most important effects of the decision was the example shown to future generations by the people of Omaha, Nebraska, who demonstrated what good can be achieved when men and women of all ages, races, creeds, nationalities, languages, occupations, economic status, and political persuasions come together for a common purpose—to bring justice to an unjust situation.

The people of Omaha set aside their various differences and united together to help right a terrible wrong. They did so for no financial renumeration or personal benefit, but simply because it was the right thing to do. These good people lit a fire throughout the nation that changed the course of history.

# 24

## The Omaha Connection

History is primarily a story of people who become connected to each other through a common purpose, event, or person. Their relationship may be short term or last for years. Some relationships change the course of history, as happened in this case.

Without the courage, commitment and kindness of this group of people, the story would have had a very different and unfavorable ending for Standing Bear and his companions:

The People of Omaha, Nebraska
Thomas Tibbles (newspaper reporter)
Bright Eyes (interpreter)
John Webster (lawyer)
Andrew Poppleton (lawyer)
Iron Eye (chief of the Omaha tribe)
Elmer Dundy (judge)
George Crook (U.S. Army general)

Standing Bear and the plight of the Poncas attracted this small group of people who came together from diverse economic, social, religious, and political backgrounds for the purpose of bringing justice to an unjust situation. They became connected not for monetary enrichment or personal ambition, but because in their heart they knew a terrible wrong had been committed that needed to be rectified. It needed to be accomplished through words and deeds, not weapons. Justice demanded nothing less. Together this small group made history. So we might ask, "What happened to this group after the trial was over?"

### The People of Omaha

The people of Omaha, Nebraska, deserve special recognition for their support of Standing Bear and the Ponca prisoners. They packed the courtroom for the trial, cheered the ruling, and donated food, supplies, and money to the

Fig. 22. Tibbles family home in Bancroft, Nebraska. Thomas (*seated left*) and Bright Eyes (*seated in upper window*). The two women may be Tibbles's daughters, Eda and May (*near front door*). Courtesy History Nebraska, RG2026-47.

Omaha Ponca Relief Committee to support the Poncas. The *Omaha Daily Herald* newspaper publicized the Ponca story and gained valuable support for reform around the nation.

Omaha clergy from various Christian denominations provided moral encouragement and leadership. The small Jewish community contributed financial support to help defray future litigation costs on behalf of the Poncas.

### Thomas Tibbles (1840–1928) and Bright Eyes (1854–1903)

Thomas Tibbles said that he heard Bright Eyes speak in an Omaha church in the fall of 1879. She was small in size, but graceful and dignified in her bearing. He could sense she was frightened, yet she composed herself and spoke clearly, as she described some of the horrors endured by Standing Bear and his family having their land taken from them and suffering through the deaths of two of his children. Bright Eyes became so moved by the story she was sharing, as well as by the intensity of the audience reaction, that she nearly fainted. Some women rushed to grab hold of her before she

Fig. 23. (*above*) Outdoor dining at the Omaha Tribe Agency, August 1901. (*Left to right*): Marguerite Diddock, Carey LaFlesche (Bright Eyes's brother), Walter Diddock (in shadow), Nettie Fremont (Bright Eyes's cousin), Marguerite Farley (facing camera at end of table). In the front row with their with their backs to the camera are Thomas Tibbles and Bright Eyes. Tibbles's family dog is behind him. Courtesy History Nebraska, RG 2737–13.

Fig. 24. (*right*) Tibbles in his study with his dog, 1908. Courtesy History Nebraska, RG2737–05.

fell, and helped her outside. The crowd sensed she had spoken from deep within her heart and cheered their approval. It was a meaningful beginning to what lay ahead.[1]

After returning home from their eastern lecture tour, Thomas Tibbles, age forty-two, and Bright Eyes, age twenty-seven, were married on June 29, 1882, in the Presbyterian Mission Church on the Omaha Reservation. They worked tirelessly together on behalf of various Ponca and Omaha tribal causes for twenty-one years until her death.[2]

In the beginning of their marriage, they lived in Tibbles's home in Omaha with his two children, Eda and May, from his first marriage to Amelia Owens Tibbles, who had died in 1879. Then, in 1883, they began to farm a quarter section of land near Bancroft, Nebraska. Bright Eyes wrote a number of articles on Indian life for national magazines. In 1893 they moved to Washington DC as newspaper correspondents for *The American Nonconformist*, an Indiana weekly paper, and for the Farmers' Alliance.

In the last years of her life, Bright Eyes became an accomplished painter, even illustrating a book about life in the Omaha tribe written by a friend. Bright Eyes died on May 26, 1903, at the age of forty-nine. She is buried in a cemetery in Bancroft, Nebraska, near her parents.[3] She was inducted in the Nebraska Hall of Fame in 1983. The inscription on her tombstone reads: "She did all that she could to make the world happier and better."

After her death Tibbles continued his work for various newspapers in Nebraska, including the *Omaha World Herald* (successor to the *Omaha Daily Herald*), and the *Independent*, a weekly Populist Party newspaper of which he was a founder in 1895. He became so active in Populist Party politics that he was chosen as the party's candidate for vice president in 1904.[4] Tibbles wrote his autobiography *Buckskin and Blanket Days* in 1905. He married Ida Belle Riddle in Ute, Iowa, in 1907. He died in Omaha on May 14, 1928, at the age of eighty-eight and is buried in a cemetery in Bellevue, Nebraska, next to his wife Ida.

### John L. Webster (1847–1929)

One of the most distinguished lawyers in Nebraska history, John L. Webster served as Omaha city attorney and general counsel for the Omaha Water Board, the Council Bluffs Street Railway Co., and the Wabash Railroad. He argued rates cases before the Interstate Commerce Commission in Washington DC and the United States Supreme Court. In 1903 he was elected president of the Nebraska Bar Association.[5] Active in Republican Party politics, he was chosen as a delegate to its national conventions in 1892 and 1896. In the process he became friends with President William McKinley.[6]

Webster played an active role in organizing the Trans-Mississippi and International Exposition, Omaha's version of a world's fair. As a member of the board of directors, he gave one of the speeches on June 1, 1898, the day the exposition opened.[7]

Webster was deeply involved in the Omaha community, serving in a variety of leadership positions for over sixty years: as a director of the Omaha Library Board alongside A. J. Poppleton, as president of the Nebraska Historical Society, and as founder of the Friends of Art Association in Nebraska. He was a great patron of the arts, bringing fine paintings to Omaha from his European travels. The civic and philanthropic organization known as Ak-Sar-Ben (Nebraska spelled backwards) honored him as their "King" in 1916 for his decades of civic and legal service to the community. The city of Omaha dedicated a street is his honor, one block from the author's family home. He died on September 2, 1929, at the age of eighty-two, and is buried in Forest Lawn Cemetery, Omaha.[8]

### Andrew J. Poppleton (1830–96)

In his memoirs, *Reminiscences*, Andrew J. Poppleton wrote that he filed the first lawsuit ever tried in the state of Nebraska, *John Pentecost v. F. M. Woods*, which concerned a land dispute on a tributary of Saddle Creek near present-day Elmwood Park in Omaha. Due to the fact that his early law practice consisted mainly of trials of land claims, he founded the Omaha Claim Club, a tribunal seeking to protect the claims of original landowners against "claim-jumpers." Poppleton continued serving as general counsel for the Union Pacific Railroad until 1888. He appeared as co-counsel with John Webster in a few other cases filed in court on behalf of the Poncas and other Native Americans. Poppleton was active in Democratic Party politics, having been its nominee for the U. S. Senate (1867) and House of Representatives (1868). He lost both elections.

Poppleton became involved in real estate development in Omaha. The "Poppleton Block" was built by him in 1886 and is today listed on the National Register of Historic Places. Like Webster, a street in Omaha is named after Poppleton. Since he had grown up on a farm in Michigan, he purchased some 1,200 acres of land near Elkhorn, Nebraska, and raised trotting horses.

Figs. 25 & 26. Two views of Omaha in the 1870s. (*Top*) Looking north from 8th and Forest Avenue, with UPRR "Cowshed" on the right. (*Bottom*) Looking northwest from Fifteenth and Douglas Streets, with the Federal Court Office under construction in the middle right. Courtesy Bostwick-Frohardt Collection owned by KM3TV and on permanent loan to the Durham Museum, Omaha, BF14-66 (*top*) and BF14-385-420E (*bottom*).

Fig. 27. Omaha in 1873. View northwest from Fourteenth and Farnam Streets facing Capitol Hill. Courtesy Bostwick-Frohardt Collection owned by KM3TV and on permanent loan to the Durham Museum, Omaha, BF14-020A.

*Reminiscences* ends with Poppleton writing: "About the first of July 1892, I became totally blind. My life of light was ended, and my life of darkness began."[9] He died on September 24, 1896, at the age of sixty-six, and is buried in Prospect Hill Cemetery in Omaha with his wife Caroline. She died in 1917 at the age of eighty-two.

### Chief Iron Eye (1818–88)

Iron Eye (Joseph LaFlesche) was a leader in the effort to provide financial support and supplies to the Poncas after their release. He was the last chief of the Omaha Tribe. Without his courage in risking arrest by riding to Fort Omaha to inform General Crook of the Ponca story, their outcome would likely have been very different. Iron Eye died on September 24, 1888, and is buried in a Cemetery in Bancroft, Nebraska, next to his wife, Mary Gale.[10]

### Elmer S. Dundy (1830–96)

Judge Elmer S. Dundy served on the Territorial Supreme Court from 1863 to 1867, when Nebraska was granted statehood. He was Nebraska's first United States District Court judge and served in that position for twenty-eight years until his death.[11] His ruling in the Standing Bear case was courageous and monumental for the Native American reform movement. Judge Dundy died on October 28, 1896, at the age of sixty-six and is buried in the Moravian Cemetery in Staten Island, New York. A county in western Nebraska is named in his honor.

### George Crook (1828–90)

On August 29, 1882, General Crook left Omaha for a reassignment to command the Military Department of Arizona. Bourke noted in his diary the reason for this move: "Indian affairs in Arizona had relapsed into a deplorable condition."[12] Crook had served the military in Arizona previously and was well respected by the Apache Tribe. As soon as he arrived in Arizona, he went into the hills to meet personally with the Apache leaders and listen to their grievances. Bourke reported that one of their leaders told him "When you were here, whenever you said a thing, we knew that it was true."[13]

Four years later, on April 28, 1886, General Crook returned to Fort Omaha and resumed command of the Department of the Platte. In 1888 he was elevated to the rank of major general of the army, and on May 4 of that year he left for Chicago to assume command of the Division of the Missouri. Crook had served nearly ten years at Fort Omaha (1875–82 and 1886–88).[14]

General George Crook died in Chicago on March 21, 1890, at the age of sixty-two. He is buried in Arlington National Cemetery. Former president Rutherford B. Hayes was a pallbearer at his funeral. Webb Hayes, son of the president, stood next to Mrs. Crook at the funeral. Webb and the general had been frequent hunting companions for many years. The Crooks treated Webb Hayes like a son since he was their godson, and because they had no children of their own.[15] Mary Crook died in 1895 and is buried alongside her husband.

Red Cloud, chief of the Ogallala Sioux, gave a fitting tribute when told of the death of General Crook: "He, at least, had never lied to us. His words gave us hope."[16]

### Summary

Thomas Tibbles, Bright Eyes, John Webster, Andrew Poppleton, Chief Iron Eye, Judge Elmer Dundy, General George Crook, and the good men, women, and clergy of Omaha united before and after the trial to support Standing Bear and the Ponca cause. They became leaders in the effort for reform.

**But there was only one leading man in this story—one Hero!**

# 25

## Standing Bear at Peace

Standing Bear (1829–1908) is the hero of this story because he had the courage to take action when no one else would.

He was a great and honorable man, a man of conviction and determination, willing to face arrest for leaving the government reservation without permission because of his love for his son and the traditions of his people.

Standing Bear was a man who fought for his freedom, not with armed resistance, but with bold action, forceful testimony, and heartfelt eloquence. He knew he and his people had been wronged. All he wanted was the right to live and die with his family on his own land—on the beloved land of his Ponca ancestors—a free man.

This is the story of the first civil rights victory for Native Americans, unprecedented in American history. For the first time a federal court declared a Native American to be a "person"—a human being, having rights and privileges to file an action for a redress of grievances in a federal court, like every other person in America.

Standing Bear won his fight for freedom. His victory began a movement of change, a slow but fundamental change. The pervading sense of "indifference" toward Native Americans, lamented by Bright Eyes and condemned by the Senate Select Committee on the Forced Removal of the Ponca Tribe, was broken. America would never be the same because of what Standing Bear did.

Everything had been taken from Standing Bear except his pride in being a Ponca. He carried in his heart the stories of the ancestors gone before him and their love of the land they called home for over two hundred years.

Standing Bear built a new home for his family on the nearly three hundred acres allotted to him by the government. He fenced his pasture for cattle and raised corn, wheat, squash, beans, and potatoes. He lived his last years surrounded by his wife Susette, her niece Lottie, and their children and grandchildren, on the land he loved, as he had always dreamed. Standing Bear died on September 3, 1908, at the age of seventy-nine.[1]

He had achieved all he had ever wanted: to live on his own land; to be buried on his own land; to live and die in peace—a free man.

### A Fitting Tribute

One hundred forty years after the decision was rendered by Judge Dundy, another historic event took place. On September 18, 2019, a beautiful majestic statue was dedicated in the United States Capitol. Artist Benjamin Victor was commissioned to sculpt a statue of Ponca chief Standing Bear to represent the state of Nebraska in Statuary Hall. Standing Bear towers over the hall with his right hand reaching out to be free with the words of his historic courtroom speech etched on either side at the base of the bronze statue.

Because of Standing Bear, a federal Judge had declared for the first time in the history of America, "That an *Indian* is a PERSON within the meaning of the laws of the United States, and has, therefore, the right to sue out a writ of habeas corpus in a federal court, or before a federal judge."[2]

Every state is allowed to place two statues in Statuary Hall to represent the history and values of its people. The fact that the state of Nebraska chose to honor an individual who was once imprisoned within its borders, considered less than a human being, who should 140 years later be put forward to the nation as a representative of its values and history, is truly a fitting tribute to this great man.

The memory of Standing Bear's courageous leadership lives on today.

Fig. 28. Chief Standing Bear bronze statue by Benjamin Victor, in Statuary Hall of the U.S. Capitol Building. Photo by Franmarie Metzler, www.house.gov.

# ACKNOWLEDGMENTS

I am grateful for the kindness of so many people who have assisted me in researching and writing this book. At the 130th anniversary celebration of the trial of Standing Bear in May 2009, Betty Davis introduced me to two people who provided invaluable insights: the late Harold Anderson, former editor and publisher of the *Omaha World Herald*, who shared with me his knowledge about General Crook and Fort Omaha; and Joe Starita, who had just published his widely acclaimed book on Standing Bear, *I Am A Man*. Thank you, Joe, for raising the profile of Standing Bear.

A very special thank you to Judi gaiashkibos, executive director of the Nebraska Commission on Indian Affairs, and a Ponca herself, who gave me an extensive interview of all things Standing Bear. Judi is the granddaughter of Otto B. Knudsen, the last chief of the Ponca Tribe. In the immediate years before Standing Bear's death, Otto Knudsen's allotment of land made him a next-door neighbor to Standing Bear. Thank you, Judi, for allowing me to use the allotment township map and for sharing stories of your family and the rich history of the Poncas. A special thank you, Judi, for all you have done to honor Chief Standing Bear with his statue in the U.S. Capitol, and the designation of the first Indigenous Peoples Day in Nebraska.

Ten years after I spoke at the 130th anniversary of the trial of Standing Bear, Kathy Aultz, current executive director of the Douglas County Historical Society, graciously invited me to give another lecture on the grounds of Fort Omaha to commemorate the 140th anniversary of the trial. A dinner followed my lecture in the Crook House. It was a memorable evening for me, coming full circle from where it all began. Thank you, Kathy. And thank you, Roxanne Knutson, for coordinating the event.

Photos are a valuable component of any historical work, so I want to give special thanks to Ana Somers and Natalie Kammerer, research specialists at the Douglas County Historical Society. Thank you, Martha Vestecka Miller of the History Nebraska Reference Department, for your patience as I searched for just the right pictures to include, and to Dell Darling of

History Nebraska. Thank you, Jillian McClenahan of Anastasia Co., for graphic designs.

Bill Gonzalez, photo archivist at the Durham Museum, which houses the unbelievable collection of mid-eighteenth to early-nineteenth-century photos in the Bostwick-Frohardt Collection, is a treasure trove of knowledge about everything concerning Omaha's early history. Special thanks, Bill, for your efforts to locate the pictures of Omaha showing the UPRR yards in the year my family emigrated from Ireland to work at that location.

I am deeply honored that I was able to interview two distinguished members of the judiciary. The Honorable Thomas K. Harmon, judge of the Douglas County Court, always made himself available to answer my questions and made valuable suggestions for further research. I am especially grateful for the time given me by the late Chief Judge Laurie Smith Camp, of the United States District Court for the District of Nebraska, one of the most knowledgeable persons on all matters concerning the trial. Her knowledge of the structure of the federal court system at the time of the trial, as well as her responses to my questions concerning why Judge Dundy may not have addressed certain issues in his ruling, were precise and to the point.

Along the way in researching this book I developed a friendship with Charles E. Wright. I was introduced to him by Scott W. Shafer of the Nebraska Commission on Indian Affairs, who felt we would have a lot in common to discuss (thanks, Scott). Charles Wright, a retired attorney with the law firm of Cline, Williams, Wright, Johnson, and Oldfather in Lincoln, Nebraska, authored *Law at Little Big Horn*. He was a tremendous source of knowledge on the legal issues involved in this case and I am grateful for his wisdom. He and his wife Suzi established a scholarship at the University of Nebraska School of Law to benefit Native American students in pursuit of a law career. Charles Wright died in 2020. He was a great blessing to me.

Many thanks to Lisa K. Headley, proofreader extraordinaire, and her husband Charles Jan Headley, my former law partner, for their support and feedback.

In July 2018 I received a call from my good friend Bruce Haney, retired financial advisor, community activist, and lifelong supporter of all people and things that add to the beauty and culture of our society. Bruce invited me to give a lecture for the New Cassel Foundation on my book, so that he could have it professionally recorded before a live audience. In order to prepare for this lecture, I realized I needed to "finish" my research of primary sources (such research never really ends) and begin the actual writing of my book. Bruce and his wife Marlene are two of our dearest friends. They have always been willing to listen and encourage me in this project. Thank you, Bruce and Marlene, for everything you have done for me.

Thank you, Cindy Patach, executive director of the New Cassel Foundation, who hosted my lecture in November 2018. It was Cindy's advertisement of the lecture in the *Omaha World Herald* that was seen by Scott W. Shafer, who then "connected" me with Charles W. Wright.

Thank you, Phil and Beth Black of The Bookworm, an independently owned bookstore in Omaha, for kindly reading my manuscript and offering helpful suggestions concerning all things that go into publishing and marketing a book in this digital age.

Thank you, Teresa A. Trumbly Lamsam, associate professor emeritus in the School of Communication, University of Nebraska–Omaha, and a member of the Osage Tribe, for reading portions of my manuscript and for your very helpful comments.

Thank you, Zachary Tilts, for ten years of asking me, "Is it done yet?" Thank you, Shelby S. Stevens, for your digital photography skills.

Special thanks to Jonathan Nitcher, interlibrary loan coordinator, Criss Library, University of Nebraska–Omaha, for hours spent locating 1879 Omaha newspapers

Thanks to my brother Thomas Dwyer for discovering in the basement of our family home a pristine edition of *Wolfe's City Directory* for the years 1878–79.

Thanks to my officemates for listening to me every day talk about this book and still showing interest: John Kellogg, Jeffrey Palzer, Julia Palzer, Rachael Kraft, and Pamela Bissell.

Thanks also to all the civic organizations and clubs who have invited me these past ten years to share Standing Bear's story with their groups throughout Iowa and Nebraska. I have been honored to share him with all of you.

Special thanks to four students of the Creighton University School of Law who clerked in our office and researched cases and treaties pertinent to this book: Bryan Carter, Tonya Whipple, Seth Moen, and Tom Schumacher. I am proud to say that today they are all distinguished practicing members of the Bar.

My very special thanks go to my friend of over forty years, John P. Mullen, a fellow of the American College of Trial Lawyers. John has read through my manuscript and its many revisions countless times and critiqued it with a "fine-tooth pen." I am grateful for his efforts in moving me away from the use of passive language (a lawyer's curse) to active shorter sentences. John's thoughtful questions led me to more research, which has made this a better book than it would have been otherwise. His comments, such as "Judges sitting in Bench Trials issue rulings, juries issue verdicts," have helped me increase the accuracy of trial terminology. Thanks, John—I could not have done this book without your help!

I have been blessed these past ten years with the support and encouragement of many people, but no one more crucial to the completion of this book than my wife of thirty-five years, Karen Kangas Dwyer, PhD, who is a professor in the School of Communications at the University of Nebraska-Omaha. In the midst of writing her own books, giving lectures, and mentoring graduate students, Karen found time to listen to my new findings, read drafts, and edit and re-edit overly long sentences. In addition to her unparalleled media publishing skills, Karen is an award-winning professor and made major contributions to the book club discussion questions. Above all, she has been moved by the injustice done to Standing Bear and the Poncas, marveled at his eloquence, and urged me to finish this important story so that all can appreciate this great man and what he did for our country. I am grateful, Karen, that you walked this journey with me. All my love!

I have lived all my life in Omaha. I attended grade school and high school on the street named after John Webster. My ancestors immigrated from Tipperary, Ireland, in 1875 to work for the Union Pacific Railroad. They lived less than twelve blocks from the federal courthouse. I often wondered why they came directly to Omaha. In researching this book, I discovered a possible answer. The Nebraska legislature created a Board of Immigration in 1870 for the specific purpose of advertising "in this country or in foreign countries" for workers to come to Omaha.[1]

My great-grandfather, Patrick Joseph Dwyer, likely read the advertisement and came to Omaha to work as a finish carpenter for the Union Pacific Railroad, at the "Cowshed." Recently my brother discovered a treasure in the basement of our family home which has been preserved for more than 140 years: *Wolfe's Omaha City Directory for 1878-79*. In the year of the Standing Bear trial, the directory listed my great-grandfather as "P. J. Dwyer, carpenter UPRR, 215 Capitol Ave."[2]

I wonder whether any of my ancestors knew the participants in the Standing Bear trial or attended the court proceedings. Was the case talked about at their evening meals? The city directory shows that Tibbles, Webster, Poppleton, Crook, and the clergy lived within a few blocks of each other and of my family.[3]

I am in awe of Standing Bear not only for his courageous leadership and integrity, but also for his acts of kindness, and for his love of family and the traditions of his people. I feel very privileged to have spent ten years getting to know and appreciate this great man. He has become a treasured friend.

# DISCUSSION QUESTIONS

### Chapter 1. His Name Was Standing Bear

1. In your opinion, what three attributes best describe Standing Bear?
2. After viewing the photograph of Standing Bear, describe your impression of his persona.

### Chapter 2. Early History of the Poncas

3. Why would the Poncas decide to settle in the Niobrara River valley?
4. Describe the importance of ancestral land to the Poncas.
5. What information did the "Notable Visitors" add to the portrayal of the Ponca tribe?

### Chapter 3. The Ponca System of Law

6. How does the meaning of the word "law" apply to the Ponca's rules of self-governance?
7. What is the basis of the Ponca's system of law?
8. Describe the purpose of the Sacred Pipe in Ponca society.
9. How do the Ponca legal process and penalties for breaking a rule of conduct reflect respect for the tribal members?

### Chapter 4. Precedents for the Ponca Removal in the American System of Law

10. What is the "doctrine of discovery?"
11. How do you think the Poncas felt when they were called "wards of the government"?
12. What negative impact did the acts of Congress have on the Poncas?

### Chapter 5. Treaties with the Poncas

13. What was the underlying principle behind the Northwest Ordinance?

14. What protection is guaranteed by Article VI of the U.S. Constitution?
15. Describe the consequences to the Poncas of the 1858 Treaty.
16. Why do you think the word "blunder" is associated with the 1868 Fort Laramie Treaty?
17. Why were the Poncas at a disadvantage in negotiating treaties with the government?

### Chapter 6. The Ponca Displacement Begins

18. Why was the buffalo so important to Native American tribes at this time?
19. How did Inspector Kemble persuade the Ponca chiefs to go with him to Indian Territory?
20. How did the Ponca Chiefs react when Inspector Kemble abandoned them in Indian Territory?
21. Describe the first time Standing Bear was arrested.
22. What finding did the Senate Select Committee on the Ponca Removal issue in 1880 concerning this episode?

### Chapter 7. Journey of Sorrows

23. Describe your feelings when you heard Standing Bear describe the loss of his home and property.
24. Describe some examples of the suffering the Poncas endured during their "Journey of Sorrows."
25. What was the condition of the Ponca people when their chiefs returned to Indian Territory after visiting with President Hayes in 1877?

### Chapter 8. Standing Bear Takes Action

26. If you were a farmer at that time and you saw these helpless Poncas come your way in the middle of winter, without food or shelter, would you help them? Why or why not?
27. What motivated Standing Bear to leave Indian Territory?
28. If you were with Standing Bear and walked all the way from Indian Territory in the middle of winter, how would you feel when you finally arrived in Nebraska?

### Chapter 9. Imprisoned at Fort Omaha

29. Why is the relationship between General Crook and Thomas Tibbles important to this story?
30. What motivated Chief Iron Eye and his daughter Bright Eyes to risk arrest in order to visit General Crook?
31. What is the "Midnight Ride"?

### Chapter 10. The Interviews

32. Why did Tibbles want to interview the Ponca prisoners?
33. What moved your heart in the Tibbles interview with the Poncas?
34. After the interview, why would Tibbles's first action be to visit Omaha churches?
35. Why would General Crook invite the Ponca prisoners into his office for an interview?
36. What effect did the Tibbles April 1, 1879, *Omaha Herald* article have nationally?

### Chapter 11. Tibbles Assembles a Legal Team

37. If you had been a lawyer in Omaha, would you have accepted or refused Tibbles's request to help the Poncas? Why?
38. How did Webster and Poppleton arrive in Omaha?

### Chapter 12. The Great Writ

39. What is the "Great Writ"?
40. Why is the Great Writ important for all Americans?
41. How did the lawyers connect the Great Writ with the newly enacted Fourteenth Amendment to the U.S. Constitution?
42. Why did the lawyers insert "separated from the tribe" into the application for the writ?
43. Where was the judge when the lawyers couldn't find him?

### Chapter 13. Witnesses Testify

44. Describe the atmosphere in the courtroom on the first day of the trial.
45. How could Commissioner Brooks's letter to District Attorney Lambertson be called callous?

46. Why was the Judge's reply to Lambertson's objection to allowing Standing Bear to testify important to the outcome of this trial?

47. Why do you think Standing Bear became so upset on the witness stand?

### Chapter 14. The Trial's Closing Arguments

48. Why was this case called a case of "firsts"?

49. Describe one key point that each lawyer made in their closing arguments.

Webster:

Lambertson:

Poppleton:

50. In your opinion, which of the three lawyers was the most persuasive? Why?

### Chapter 15. Standing Bear's Historic Speech

51. Who is Bright Eyes and why is she so important to this moment in the trial?

52. Why was the opportunity to speak in the courtroom so important for Standing Bear's "quest for freedom"?

53. What gestures did Standing Bear employ in his speech that conveyed the emotions that were stirring in his heart?

54. How would Standing Bear's statement "I am a Man" have affected you if you had been in the courtroom that day?

### Chapter 16. A Time for Waiting

55. If you had been in attendance during the two-day trial, what would you tell your family, friends, or fellow students about what it was like to witness it all?

56. Describe what emotions the Poncas must have been feeling during the week of waiting.

57. Discuss what was at stake for Standing Bear, the Ponca prisoners, all Native Americans, and our nation itself as everyone awaited the judge's decision.

*Chapter 17. The Court's Decision*

58. Do the opening remarks of Judge Dundy convey the emotions and struggle he faced, and why did he take a full ten days to issue his decision?
59. What three issues did Judge Dundy highlight in his ruling?
60. Why was it so important for Judge Dundy to begin his ruling, "That an Indian is a person within the meaning of the law of the United States"?

*Chapter 18. Standing Bear Keeps His Promise*

61. How disappointed was Standing Bear when his initial efforts to bury the bones of his son Bear Shield failed?
62. After enduring such great suffering, how would Standing Bear, his wife, and friends have felt when they were finally able to bury Bear Shield on Ponca ancestral land?

*Chapter 19. Standing Bear's Gratitude and Generosity*

63. What three gifts did Standing Bear give Tibbles, Webster, and Poppleton?
64. What do Standing Bear's gifts of personal items indicate about his character?

*Chapter 20. A Fire Kindled*

65. What was the purpose of the Omaha Ponca Relief Committee?
66. Where did Bright Eyes give her first public speech, and what was the reaction?
67. Why did Tibbles, Bright Eyes, and Standing Bear travel to the East Coast?
68. Who was Helen Hunt Jackson and what was her contribution to the Indian Reform Movement?

*Chapter 21. Redress for Wrongs*

69. What result did the two government investigations have on the Poncas?
70. What are your feelings when you see the picture of Standing Bear and his family on their own land?

### Chapter 22. The Standing Bear Decision Sets Legal Precedent

71. What is the importance of the *John Elk* lawsuit in relationship to the Standing Bear decision?
72. Has the Standing Bear decision been cited in other court cases as authoritative law?

### Chapter 23. A Nation Aroused from the Sin of Indifference

73. What does Bright Eyes mean by the "sin of indifference"?
74. List seven examples of the impact the Standing Bear decision had on the nation.

### Chapter 24. The Omaha Connection

75. What does the word "connection" mean to this story?
76. Explain how diversity among the people of Omaha was important to the outcome of Standing Bear's quest for freedom.
77. What issues today could be solved if people from diverse backgrounds came together like these Omaha people did nearly a century and a half ago?

### Chapter 25. Standing Bear at Peace

78. Why is Standing Bear the hero of this story?
79. Why is this case considered the first civil rights victory for Native Americans?
80. What is your reaction to the state of Nebraska placing a statue of Standing Bear in the U.S. Capitol as one of two statues that represent Nebraska?

### Final Questions

1. What does it mean that Standing Bear won his quest for freedom?
2. Why is Standing Bear one of the most important people in American history?

# NOTES

## Preface

1. For more information on the "Indian Territory," see Dianna Everett, "Indian Territory," *The Encyclopedia of Oklahoma History and Culture*, https://www.okhistory.org/publications/enc/entry.php?entry=IN018.

2. *Omaha Daily Herald*, April 13, 1879.

3. Olson, *History of Nebraska*, 13, 35.

## 1. His Name Was Standing Bear

1. Bourke, *Diaries*, 3:180.

2. *Omaha Daily Herald*, May 2, 1879.

## 2. Early History of the Poncas

1. J. Howard, *The Ponca Tribe*, 14.

2. Dorsey, *Migrations of Siouan Tribes*, 215. For an updated analysis of the early history of the Poncas see Ritter, *Piercing Together the Ponca Past: Reconstructing Degiha Migrations to the Great Plains*, 272–73.

3. Fletcher and LaFlesche, *The Omaha Tribe*, 1:35. See Bourke, *Diaries*, 3:182, for the quote Standing Bear made in his interview with General Crook, March 31, 1879.

4. Dorsey, 215.

5. Dorsey, *Migrations of Siouan Tribes*, 215; J. Howard, *The Ponca Tribe*, 15.

6. Dorsey, *Migrations of Siouan Tribes*, 215; J. Howard, *The Ponca Tribe*, 15.

7. Nebraska was admitted to the Union on March 1, 1867. South Dakota and North Dakota were admitted to the Union on November 2, 1889.

8. Dorsey, *Migrations of Siouan Tribes*, 219.

9. Dorsey, *Migrations of Siouan Tribes*, 219.

10. Capps, *The Old West*, 74–75.

11. DeMallie, *The First Voices*, 60–61.

12. J. Howard, *The Ponca Tribe*, 19.

13. J. Howard, *The Ponca Tribe*, 8.

14. Fletcher and LaFlesche, *The Omaha Tribe*, 1:95–99. Standing Bear's testimony before the Senate Select Committee, 11, is a good source for the types of crops generally planted by the Poncas.

15. Moulton, *The Definitive Journals*, 3: 49–50.

16. Moulton, *The Definitive Journals*, 3:399–400.

17. Catlin, *Letters and Notes*, 1:ix.

18. Catlin, *Letters and Notes*, 212.

19. Schach, "Maximilian, Prince of Wied," 12–13.

20. Carlson, *The Plains Indians*, 12.

21. Moulton, *The Definitive Journals*, 3: 399–400.

### 3. The Ponca System of Law

1. State v. Central Lumber Co., 123 N.W. 504 (S.D. 1909).

2. J. Howard, *The Ponca Tribe*, 16.

3. J. Howard, *The Ponca Tribe*, 19.

4. J. Howard, *The Ponca Tribe*, 19.

5. Testimony of Standing Bear, U.S. Congress, *Senate Select Committee Report*, 17.

6. Fletcher and LaFlesche, *The Omaha Tribe*, 1:269.

7. J. Howard, *The Ponca Tribe*, 91; Fletcher and LaFlesche, *The Omaha Tribe*, 1:208–9.

8. J. Howard, *The Ponca Tribe*, 91; Fletcher and LaFlesche, *The Omaha Tribe*, 1:47–48.

9. Fletcher and LaFlesche, *The Omaha Tribe*, 1:213.

10. J. Howard, *The Ponca Tribe*, 96.

11. J. Howard, *The Ponca Tribe*, 96.

12. Fletcher and LaFlesche, *The Omaha Tribe*, 1:215.

13. J. Howard, *The Ponca Tribe*, 95.

14. J. Howard, *The Ponca Tribe*, 95.

### 4. Precedents for Removal

1. Johnson and Graham's Lessee v. William M'Intosh, 21 U.S. 543 (1823). John Marshall, who wrote the decision in the Johnson case, was born in 1755 in Virginia. After serving in the Revolutionary War, he was elected to the Virginia Legislature and later to Congress. He never went to law school, but did attend lectures given by America's first law professor, George Wythe, at the College of William & Mary. After practicing law for fifteen years and managing his family farm, he was appointed chief justice of the United States Supreme Court in 1801 by President John Adams. He served in that position for thirty-four years until his death in 1835.

2. Johnson and Graham's Lessee v. William M'Intosh.

3. Johnson and Graham's Lessee v. William M'Intosh. Justice Marshall's declaration that "it has never been doubted" is challenged by the actions of the founder of Rhode Island, Roger Williams, who "purchased his land from the Indians," the Narragansett tribe. Miller, *Roger Williams*, 51.

4. See "Closing Argument of John L. Webster," chapter 14 of this book. For a thorough analysis of the Johnson case and the long-lasting negative effects of the "doctrine of discovery" upheld by Justice Marshall, see Watson, *Buying America*.

5. The Cherokee Nation v. The State of Georgia, 30 U.S. 1. (1831). *Black's Law Dictionary* defines the term *pupilage/pupillus* to mean "a person under the authority of a tutor," 1234.

6. Even though the Declaration of Independence is not part of the law, it certainly was a source of inspiration to Abraham Lincoln in his Gettysburg Address, and a guide for the framers of the Fourteenth Amendment.

7. Prucha, *The Great Father*, 111.

8. Utley, *The Indian Frontier*, 41–43; Wishart, *An Unspeakable Sadness*, 55.

9. U.S. Congress, Indian Removal Act .

10. Capps, *The Old West*, 25.

11. Remini, *Life of Andrew Jackson*, 112.

12. U.S. Congress, Kansas-Nebraska Act of 1854.

13. U.S. Congress, Homestead Act of 1862.

## 5. Treaties with the Poncas

1. Ordinance for the Government, Sec. 14. Art. 3.

2. Wright, *Little Big Horn*, 66.

3. *Black's Law Dictionary*, 1645.

4. *Black's Law Dictionary*, 1643.

5. *Black's Law Dictionary*, 1641.

6. *Black's Law Dictionary*, 1641.

7. United States v. Schooner Peggy, 5 U.S. 103, 109–10, 2 L. Ed. 49, 51 (1801).

8. National Archives. American Indian Treaties: Catalog Links.

9. Ponca Treaty of 1817. William Clark is the same man who entered the Ponca village in 1804 on the Lewis and Clark Expedition. Chouteau was a member of the famous St. Louis family who controlled much of the trading with the Great Plains tribes for many years.

10. Nichols, *General Henry Atkinson*, 97–98.

11. Ponca Treaty of 1825, Article 3.

12. Wishart, *Unspeakable Sadness*, 27, 133.

13. Carlson, *The Plains Indians*, 8; Wishart, *Encyclopedia*, 184–85.

14. Ponca Treaty of 1858, Article 2.

15. Ponca Treaty of 1858, Article 1.

16. *Report of the Commissioner.*

17. Ponca Treaty of 1865, Article 2.

18. Ponca Treaty of 1865, Article 2.

19. Brule Treaty of 1868, Article 2.

20. Sheldon, *History and Stories*, 223.

21. U.S. Congress, *Senate Select Committee Report*, 5.

22. Indian Appropriation Act.

23. Prucha, *The Great Father*, 164.

24. Capps, *The Old West*, 155.

25. Hoig, *White Man's Paper Trail*, 180.

26. Testimony of Rev. William H. Hare. U.S. Congress, *Senate Select Committee Report*, 117.

## 6. Ponca Displacement Begins

1. Prucha, *The Great Father*, 180.

2. Prucha, *The Great Father*, 180.

3. Prucha, *The Great Father*, 174.

4. Fletcher and LaFlesche, *The Omaha Tribe*, 1:290-311.

5. Fletcher and LaFlesche, *The Omaha Tribe*, 2:635.

6. Testimony of Rev. James Owen Dorsey given to the Ponca Commission, January 1881, found in Bourke, *Diaries*, 4:223-25. *Senate Select Committee Report*, 382-95, provided numerous letters and reports from government officials verifying the constant Brule attacks on the Poncas during the 1870s.

7. Testimony of Rev. James Owen Dorsey given to the Ponca Commission, January 1881, found in Bourke's *Diaries*, 4:225-27.

8. U.S. Congress, *Senate Select Committee Report*, 122-23.

9. *Bismarck Tribune*, August 12, 1874.

10. Anderson, "Black Hills Exclusion Policy," 1. There was a provision in the Fort Laramie Treaty that excluded anyone from trespassing on these Sioux lands. To avoid a battle with the Sioux, the government arrested a trespasser named John Gordon, the leader of a group of gold-seeking miners. Gordon's attorney filed a writ of habeas corpus that was heard in the federal courthouse in Omaha before Judge Elmer S. Dundy in the summer of 1875.

11. Wright, *Little Big Horn*, 82-89. See United States v. Sioux Nation of Indians, 448 U.S. 371 (1980), for a discussion of these facts in reference to a contested action for compensation filed earlier by the Sioux in the United States Court of Claims.

12. Bourke, *On the Border*, 232.

13. Testimony of Kemble, U.S. Congress, *Senate Select Committee Report*, 49-50.

14. Testimony of Standing Bear, U.S. Congress, *Senate Select Committee Report*, 3.

15. Testimony of Standing Bear, U.S. Congress, *Senate Select Committee Report*, 4.

16. Testimony of Standing Bear, U.S. Congress, *Senate Select Committee Report*, 13.

17. Testimony of Standing Bear, U.S. Congress, *Senate Select Committee Report*, 5.

18. Testimony of Kemble, U.S. Congress, *Senate Select Committee Report*, 52.

19. Testimony of Standing Bear, U.S. Congress, *Senate Select Committee Report*, 18.

20. U.S. Congress, *Report of the Commission*, 14.

21. *Arkansas City Traveler*, February 21, 1877.

22. *Arkansas City Traveler*, February 21, 1877.

23. Jackson, *A Century of Dishonor*, chapter 6; Testimony of Standing Bear, U.S. Congress, *Senate Select Committee Report*, 6-7.

24. Testimony of Bright Eyes, U.S. Congress, *Senate Select Committee Report*, 22.

25. Testimony of Bright Eyes, U.S. Congress, *Senate Select Committee Report*, 23.

26. Testimony of Bright Eyes, U.S. Congress, *Senate Select Committee Report*, 23

27. Testimony of Bright Eyes, U.S. Congress, *Senate Select Committee Report*, 23.

28. Testimony of Bright Eyes, U.S. Congress, *Senate Select Committee Report*, 23.

29. *Sioux City Journal*, March 31, 1877.

30. Jackson, *A Century of Dishonor*, chapter 6. The *Senate Select Committee Report* in 1880 included testimony that "Kemble caused rations to be withheld from all those members of the tribe who refused to go." U.S. Congress, *Senate Select Committee Report*, 12–13.

31. U.S. Congress, *Senate Select Committee Report*, 7, 12.

32. U.S. Congress, *Senate Select Committee Report*, 8.

## 7. Journey of Sorrows

1. Phillips, *The Indian Ring*, 345–67.

2. U.S. Department of the Interior, *Annual Report of the Secretary of the Interior for 1877*, includes "Journal of the March" by E. A. Howard, 95.

3. Tibbles, *The Ponca Chiefs*, 13; Testimony of Standing Bear. U.S. Congress, *Senate Select Committee Report*, 1.

4. *Boston Daily Advertiser*, December 10, 1879.

5. Testimony of Tibbles, U.S. Congress, *Senate Select Committee Report*, 41.

6. Testimony of White Eagle, U.S. Congress, *Senate Select Committee Report*, 78.

7. Fletcher and LaFlesche, *The Omaha Tribe* 1:51.

8. U.S. Department of the Interior, *Annual Report of the Secretary of the Interior for 1877*, includes Journal of the March by E. A. Howard, 96.

9. Testimony of White Eagle, U.S. Congress, *Senate Select Committee Report*, 15.

10. U.S. Department of the Interior, *Annual Report of the Secretary of the Interior for 1877*, includes Journal of the March by E. A. Howard, 97–99.

11. *Omaha World Herald*, December 3, 2013.

12. Testimony of Bright Eyes, U.S. Congress, *Senate Select Committee Report*, 24; Green, *Iron Eye's Family*, 57.

13. U.S. Department of the Interior, *Annual Report of the Secretary of the Interior for 1877*, includes Journal of the March by E. A. Howard, 97.

14. U.S. Department of the Interior, *Annual Report of the Secretary of the Interior for 1877*, includes Journal of the March by E. A. Howard, 100.

15. U.S. Department of the Interior, *Annual Report of the Secretary of the Interior for 1877*, includes Journal of the March by E. A. Howard, 101.

16. Testimony of Standing Bear, U.S. Congress, *Senate Select Committee Report*, 12, 20.

17. U.S. Congress, *Senate Select Committee Report*, 14.

18. *Omaha Daily Herald*, April 1, 1879; Testimony of Standing Bear, U.S. Congress, *Senate Select Committee Report*, 10.

19. U.S. Congress, *Report of The Commission*, 16.

20. U.S. Congress, *Senate Select Committee Report*, 8.

21. The Cherokee Nation v. The State of Georgia.

## 8. Standing Bear Takes Action

1. Tibbles, *The Ponca Chiefs*, 83.

2. J. Howard, *The Ponca Tribe*, 93.

3. Tibbles, *The Ponca Chiefs*, 15.

4. Tibbles, *The Ponca Chiefs*; Testimony of Standing Bear, U.S. Congress, *Senate Select Committee Report*, 16.

5. Tibbles, *The Ponca Chiefs*, 16.

6. Bourke, *On the Border*, 427.

7. Tibbles, *The Ponca Chiefs*, 43.

8. Tibbles, *The Ponca Chiefs*, 43. Jacob Vore was Indian Agent to the Omaha Tribe from 1876 to 1879.

9. Tibbles, *The Ponca Chiefs*, 43.

10. Tibbles, *The Ponca Chiefs*, 44.

11. Tibbles, *The Ponca Chiefs*, 16.

12. Tibbles, *The Ponca Chiefs*, 55, reproducing a letter from Rev. Dorsey to Col. Meacham.

13. Testimony of Bright Eyes, U.S. Congress. *Senate Select Committee Report*, 29.

## *9. Imprisoned at Fort Omaha*

1. Tibbles, *The Ponca Chiefs*, 41.

2. Tibbles, *The Ponca Chiefs*, 41.

3. Wolfe, *Omaha City Directory 1878-79*, 121. Until the fall of 1879, George and Mary Crook lived at 596 Eighteenth Street in downtown Omaha. Crook married Mary Tapscott Dailey on August 22, 1865.

4. Douglas County Historical Society. *Crook House Tour Guide*; Bourke's *Diaries*, 3:342-43.

5. For more information, see www.DouglasCountyHistory.org.

6. Douglas County Historical Society. *Crook House Tour Guide*; Wolfe, *Omaha City Directory 1878-79*, 73; *Fort Omaha Walking Tour*.

7. Douglas County Historical Society. *Crook House Tour Guide*.

8. Testimony of Bright Eyes, U.S. Congress, *Senate Select Committee Report*, 36.

9. Fletcher and LaFlesche, *The Omaha Tribe* 2:635.

10. Dando-Collins, *Standing Bear*, 50-54, 240-41. I concur with Dando-Collins's belief that there could be no other credible source for General Crook's knowledge of the Ponca story than Chief Iron Eye and Bright Eyes. It is possible that they made the hundred-mile journey on horseback within a twenty-four-hour period. However, to avoid the risk of being arrested for leaving their reservation without government permission, they likely rode during the night hours and rested themselves and their horses during the day. So a one-and-a-half-day trip makes more sense. Also, whether they stayed somewhere in Omaha after the meeting with Tibbles ended at 4:30 a.m. or started on their journey home is unknown. The longer they stayed in Omaha, the greater their chance of being arrested unless General Crook issued them a pass. At some point they must have been granted a pass by General Crook or by some other

government official since they were in the courtroom during the trial and were in Omaha when the decision was rendered.

11. Worcester, "Friends of the Indian," 278–81.

12. Wolfe, *Omaha City Directory 1878–79*, 227.

13. Tibbles, *The Ponca Chiefs*, 18–19.

14. Tibbles, *The Ponca Chiefs*, 18.

15. Tibbles, *The Ponca Chiefs*, 31. General Crook's prior knowledge was confirmed in Bourke's *Diary*, 3:184.

16. Wolfe, *Omaha City Directory 1878–79*, 121; Wilson, *Nebraska Historical Tour Guide* 22.

17. Sheldon, *History and Stories*, 231.

## 10. The Interviews

1. Tibbles, *The Ponca Chiefs*, 19.

2. Tibbles, *Buckskin*, 187.

3. Tibbles, *Ponca Chiefs*, 18; Bourke, *Diaries* 3:492.

4. Tibbles, *Ponca Chiefs*, 19.

5. *Omaha Daily Herald*, April 1, 1879.

6. *Omaha Daily Herald*, April 1, 1879.

7. *Omaha Daily Herald*, April 1, 1879.

8. *Omaha Daily Herald*, April 1, 1879.

9. *Omaha Daily Herald*, April 1, 1879.

10. *Omaha Daily Herald*, April 1, 1879.

11. *Omaha Daily Herald*, April 1, 1879.

12. *Omaha Daily Herald*, April 1, 1879.

13. *Omaha Daily Herald*, April 1, 1879.

14. *Omaha Daily Herald*, April 1, 1879.

15. *Omaha Daily Herald*, April 1, 1879.

16. Tibbles, *Buckskin*, 196. According to the *Omaha City Directory 1878–79*, 36–37, all Sunday services at all four churches named in the telegram were 10:30 a.m. and 7:30 p.m.

17. Tibbles, *The Ponca Chiefs*, 27–28.

18. Tibbles, *The Ponca Chiefs*, 28.

19. Bourke, *Diaries*, 3:185. For a thorough analysis of Bourke's life and work see Porter, *Paper Medicine Man*.

20. Bourke, *Diaries*, 3:180.

21. Bourke, *Diaries*, 3:180.

22. Bourke, *Diaries*, 3:180.

23. Bourke, *Diaries*, 3:182.

24. Bourke, *Diaries*, 3:183.

23. Bourke, *Diaries*, 3:185.

26. Bourke, *Diaries*, 3:185.

27. Tibbles, *The Ponca Chiefs*, 32.

28. Tibbles, *The Ponca Chiefs*, 33. The April 1 and 2, 1879, editions of the *Chicago Tribune* contained lengthy articles on the editorial pages. Even though their source was Tibbles's articles, the headline in the April 1 edition was titled "Hardship" and contained five subheadings, including "The Unhappy Ponca Indians Hold a Council with Gen. Crook" "Their People Stricken and Die, and There is No Help," and "Gen. Crook Full of Sorrow for the Victims, but Ready to Obey Orders."

29. *Omaha Daily Herald*, April 1, 1879.

30. *Omaha Daily Herald*, April 1, 1879.

## 11. Tibbles Assembles a Team

1. Wolfe, *Omaha City Directory 1878-79*, 296–97. Omaha's population would soar to just over a hundred thousand by 1900, according to Larsen and Cottrell, *The Gate City*, 37, 122.

2. Wolfe, *Omaha City Directory 1878-79*, 284; *Omaha Sun*, August 7, 1975.

3. Tibbles, *The Ponca Chiefs*, 34.

4. Tibbles, *The Ponca Chiefs*, 34.

5. Tibbles, *The Ponca Chiefs*, 35.

6. Tibbles, *The Ponca Chiefs*, 35.

7. Tibbles, *The Ponca Chiefs*, 35; Wolfe, *Omaha City Directory 1878-79*, 237.

8. A. Poppleton, *Reminiscences*, 32.

9. Wolfe, *Omaha City Directory 1878-79*, 237; Poppleton, *Reminiscences*, 9; Douglas County Historical Society, *The Banner* (Dec. 2008), 11. As the first lawyer to open a law practice in Omaha, Poppleton also led the way in advertising his services. The following ad was placed in the *Omaha Times*, February 10, 1859: "Andrew J. Poppleton and George E. Lake, attorneys at law. Dealers in land warrants and exchanges, loan and collection agents, Omaha, Nebraska."

10. Snoddy, *Their Man in Omaha*, 1:656.

## 12. The Great Writ

1. A. Poppleton, *Reminiscences*, 32.

2. Tibbles, *The Ponca Chiefs*, 34–35.

3. *Black's Law Dictionary*, 1647.

4. U.S. Congress, *Report of the Committee*, 10.

5. *Black's Law Dictionary*, 709.

6. Fay v. Noia, 372 U.S. 391, 401–02 (1963). Other cases discussing the Writ are: Peyton v. Rowe, 391 U.S. 54 (1968); Smith v. O'Grady, 313 U.S. 329 (1941); Preiser v. Rodriguez, 411 U.S. 475 (1973); Kidd v. Norman, 651 F.3d 947 (8th Cir. 2011)

7. Danziger and Gillingham, *1215*, 83.

8. Blackstone, *Commentaries*, 437; Parliament of England, Habeas Corpus Act.

9. Blackstone, *Commentaries*, 438.

10. *Black's Law Dictionary*, 1642.

11. U.S. Congress, Judiciary Act of 1789.

12. *Ex parte* Merryman, 17 F. Cas. 144 (Md. 1861).

13. U.S. Congress, Habeas Corpus Suspension Act.

14. U.S. Congress, Habeas Corpus Act.

15. *Application of Ma-chu-nah-zha*, April 8, 1879, and Return of General Crook, April 11, 1879, full text available in Tibbles, *The Ponca Chiefs*, 36.

16. *Application of Ma-chu-nah-zha*, April 8, 1879, and Return of General Crook, April 11, 1879, full text available in Tibbles, *The Ponca Chiefs*, 36.

17. *Application of Ma-chu-nah-zha*, April 8, 1879, and Return of General Crook, April 11, 1879, full text available in Tibbles, *The Ponca Chiefs*, 37.

18. *Application of Ma-chu-nah-zha*, April 8, 1879, and Return of General Crook, April 11, 1879, full text available in Tibbles, *The Ponca Chiefs*, 37.

19. *Application of Ma-chu-nah-zha*, April 8, 1879, and Return of General Crook, April 11, 1879, full text available in Tibbles, *The Ponca Chiefs*, 38.

20. *Application of Ma-chu-nah-zha*, April 8, 1879, and Return of General Crook, April 11, 1879, full text available in Tibbles, *The Ponca Chiefs*, 38–39.

21. Tibbles, *Buckskin*, 199.

22. *Application of Ma-chu-nah-zha*.

23. The Writ, Douglas County Historical Society, 6–7.

24. *Omaha Daily Herald*, May 2, 1879.

25. Tibbles, *The Ponca Chiefs*, 46–48.

26. Tibbles, *The Ponca Chiefs*, 49.

27. Tibbles, *The Ponca Chiefs*, 49.

28. Tibbles, *The Ponca Chiefs*, 50.

29. Tibbles, *The Ponca Chiefs*, 53–54.

30. Tibbles, *The Ponca Chiefs*, 54.

31. Wunder and Scherer, *Echo of Its Time*, 55.

### 13. *Witnesses Testify*

1. Bourke, *Diaries*, 3:187.

2. *Omaha Daily Herald*, May 2, 1879.

3. Wolfe, *Omaha City Directory 1878–79*, 35.

4. Wolfe, *Omaha City Directory 1878–79*, 296–313,

5. Wolfe, *Omaha City Directory 1878–79*, 307.

6. Reilly, *Bound to Have Blood*, 98–110. According to Wolfe's *City Directory*, Omaha was awash with newspapers. There were four daily/weekly English newspapers in Omaha at the time of the trial: (1) the *Omaha Daily Herald* (ODH), founded in 1865, George L. Miller, editor, located at 257 Farnam Street (at the time of the trial, the front page of this newspaper identified itself as the *Omaha Herald*; whereas, the editorial page of the paper identified itself as the *Omaha Daily Herald*); (2) the *Omaha Bee*, founded in 1871, Edward Rosewater, editor, located at 138 Farnam

Street; (3) the *Omaha Republican*, founded in 1858, D. C. Brooks, editor, located at 220 Douglas Street; and (4) the *Omaha Evening News*, J. C. Wheeler, editor, located at 521 Thirteenth Street. Omaha also had three newspapers published only once a week in English. In addition there was one German weekly, one Bohemian weekly, and one Danish weekly (Wolfe, *City Directory*, 307). In 1885 Gilbert M. Hitchcock founded the *Omaha Evening World*. In 1889 he purchased the *Omaha Herald*, and the two papers merged into the *Omaha World Herald*.

7. Brown, "George L. Miller," 282.

8. Brown, "George L. Miller," 277.

9. Tibbles, *Buckskin*, 200.

10. Tibbles, *Buckskin*, 197.

11. *Omaha Daily Herald*, May 2, 1879.

12. *Omaha Daily Herald*, May 2, 1879.

13. *Omaha Daily Herald*, May 2, 1879. A demurrer is an allegation of a defendant saying that even if all the factual allegations made in the plaintiff's petition are true, they are not sufficient to establish a valid cause of action for the plaintiff to proceed with, or to force the defendant to have to answer. Today the Federal Rules of Procedure do not provide for the use of the demurrer, but provide for the use of something similar—a motion to dismiss. *Black's Law Dictionary*, 432–33.

14. *Omaha Daily Herald*, May 2, 1879.

15. Department of the Interior, Letter of E. A. Brooks, 1.

16. Department of the Interior, Letter of E. A. Brooks, 3.

17. Department of the Interior, Letter of E. A. Brooks, 5.

18. *Omaha Daily Herald*, May 2, 1879.

19. *Omaha Daily Herald*, May 2, 1879.

20. *Omaha Daily Herald*, May 2, 1879; Tibbles, *The Ponca Chiefs*, 66–67.

21. *Omaha Daily Herald*, May 2, 1879.

22. Tibbles, *The Ponca Chiefs*, 68.

23. Tibbles, *The Ponca Chiefs*, 69.

24. Tibbles, *The Ponca Chiefs*, 69–70.

25. Tibbles, *The Ponca Chiefs*, 71.

26. Tibbles, *The Ponca Chiefs*, 72.

27. Tibbles, *The Ponca Chiefs*, 73

28. Tibbles, *The Ponca Chiefs*, 69–70.

29. Tibbles, *The Ponca Chiefs*, 77.

30. Tibbles, *The Ponca Chiefs*, 78.

31. Tibbles, *The Ponca Chiefs*, 79.

32. *Omaha Daily Herald*, May 2, 1879.

33. *Omaha Daily Herald*, May 2, 1879.

34. The Cherokee Nation v. The State of Georgia.

35. *Omaha Daily Herald*, May 2, 1879.

36. *Black's Law Dictionary*, 1603.

37. *Omaha Daily Herald*, May 2, 1879.

38. *Omaha Daily Herald*, May 2, 1879.

39. *Omaha Daily Herald*, May 2, 1879.

40. *Omaha Daily Herald*, May 2, 1879

41. Tibbles, *The Ponca Chiefs*, 83–84.

42. *Omaha Daily Herald*, May 2, 1879

43. *Omaha Daily Herald*, May 2, 1879.

44. *Omaha Daily Herald*, May 2, 1879.

45. Tibbles, *The Ponca Chiefs*, 91.

46. *Omaha Daily Herald*, May 2, 1879.

47. *Omaha Daily Herald*, May 2, 1879.

## 14. *Trial's Closing Arguments*

1. Tibbles, *Buckskin*, 200.

2. *New York Times*, May 2, 1879.

3. The Cherokee Nation v. The State of Georgia.

4. *Omaha Daily Herald*, May 2, 1879.

5. *Omaha Daily Herald*, May 2, 1879; *Omaha Daily Herald*, May 3, 1879.

6. *Omaha Daily Herald*, May 3, 1879.

7. *Omaha Daily Herald*, May 3, 1879.

8. *Omaha Daily Herald*, May 3, 1879.

9. *Omaha Daily Herald*, May 4, 1879.

10. A. Poppleton, *Reminiscences*, 32.

11. *Omaha Daily Herald*, May 3, 1879.

12. *Omaha Daily Herald*, May 3, 1879.

13. *Omaha Daily Herald*, May 3, 1879.

14. *Omaha Daily Herald*, May 3, 1879.

15. *Omaha Daily Herald*, May 3, 1879.

16. *Omaha Daily Herald*, May 4, 1879.

17. *Omaha Daily Herald*, May 3, 1879.

18. *Omaha Daily Herald*, May 3, 1879.

19. *Omaha Daily Herald*, May 3, 1879.

20. *Omaha Daily Herald*, May 3, 1879.

21. *Omaha Daily Herald*, May 3, 1879.

22. U.S. Congress, *Report of the Committee*.

23. *Omaha Daily Herald*, May 3, 1879.

24. *Omaha Daily Herald*, May 3, 1879.

25. *Omaha Daily Herald*, May 3, 1879.

26. Dred Scott v. Sandford, 60 U.S. 393 (1856).

27. *Omaha Daily Herald*, May 7, 1879.

28. *Cases Determined*, 5:456.

29. *Cases Determined*, 5:456.

30. A. Poppleton, *Reminiscences*, 32. Poppleton had a very close relationship with his wife Caroline, as evident in his statement: "Looking back nearly forty years I can see very plainly that without her my life might have become largely valueless and useless. She has been my stay and support and anchor in every worthy purpose and achievement." *Reminiscences*, 12.

31. *Omaha Daily Herald*, May 4, 1879.

32. *Omaha Daily Herald*, May 4, 1879.

33. *Omaha Daily Herald*, May 4, 1879.

34. *Omaha Daily Herald*, May 4, 1879.

35. *Omaha Daily Herald*, May 4, 1879.

36. *Omaha Daily Herald*, May 4, 1879.

37. *Omaha Daily Herald*, May 4, 1879.

38. *Omaha Daily Herald*, May 4, 1879.

39. *Omaha Daily Herald*, May 4, 1879.

40. *Omaha Daily Herald*, May 6, 1879.

41. *Omaha Daily Herald*, May 6, 1879.

42. *Omaha Daily Herald*, May 6, 1879.

43. *Omaha Daily Herald*, May 7, 1879.

44. *Omaha Daily Herald*, May 7, 1879.

45. *Omaha Daily Herald*, May 3, 1879.

### 15. Standing Bear's Speech

1. *Omaha Daily Herald*, May 3, 1879.

2. Sheldon, *History and Stories*, 229–30.

3. Bourke, *On the Border*, 428.

4. *Omaha Daily Herald*, May 3, 1879.

5. *Omaha Daily Herald*, May 3, 1879.

6. *Omaha Daily Herald*, May 3, 1879.

7. Tibbles, *Buckskin*, 201.

8. Standing Bear employed a similar metaphor during his interview in General Crook's office on March 31, 1879, Bourke, *Diaries*, 3:183. The metaphor can be found in its entirety in Tibbles, *Buckskin*, 200–201.Tibbles did not include the metaphor in his May 4, 1879, newspaper report, possibly to protect the reputation of Judge Dundy from the public who were not in the courtroom that day to see and hear Standing Bear point to the judge saying, "You are that man." The judge said in his ruling that he was acutely aware that he would be criticized either way. So Tibbles may have felt recording what Standing Bear said about the judge could have created a public outcry of disrespect for the court, and made it more difficult for Judge Dundy to rule in favor of the prisoners. Note: The *Omaha Republican* for May 4, 1879 is similar in many respects to the account given in the *Omaha Herald* of the same date; however, it fails to include Standing Bear's metaphor.

9. *Omaha Daily Herald*, May 4, 1879.

10. *Omaha Daily Herald*, May 3, 1879.

11. C. Poppleton, *The War Bonnet*, 2.

## 16. A Time for Waiting

1. Tibbles, *The Ponca Chiefs*, 65.

2. *Cases Determined*, 5:461.

3. Tocqueville, *Democracy in America*, 123.

4. A. Poppleton, *Reminiscences*, 32.

## 17. The Court's Decision

1. *Omaha Daily Herald*, May 13, 1879.

2. *Cases Determined*, 5:453–69.

3. *St Louis Republican*, quoted in *The Commonwealth*, Topeka, Kansas, May 15, 1879, 2.

4. Testimony of Bright Eyes, U.S. Congress, *Senate Select Committee Report*, 30.

5. *Cases Determined*, 5:454.

6. *Cases Determined*, 5:454.

7. *Cases Determined*, 5:455.

8. *Cases Determined*, 5:457.

9. *Cases Determined*, 5:457.

10. *Cases Determined*, 5:458.

11. *Cases Determined*, 5:458.

12. *Cases Determined*, 5:459.

13. *Cases Determined*, 5:459.

14. *Black's Law Dictionary*, 1057.

15. *Cases Determined*, 5:459.

16. *Cases Determined*, 5:460.

17. *Cases Determined*, 5:460.

18. *Cases Determined*, 5:461.

19. *Cases Determined*, 5:462.

20. *Cases Determined*, 5:463.

21. *Cases Determined*, 5:463.

22. *Cases Determined*, 5:464.

23. *Cases Determined*, 5:464.

24. *Cases Determined*, 5:464.

25. *Cases Determined*, 5:467.

26. *Cases Determined*, 5:465.

27. *Cases Determined*, 5:466.

28. *Cases Determined*, 5:466–67.

29. *Cases Determined*, 5:467.

30. *Cases Determined*, 5:467.

31. *Cases Determined*, 5:468.

32. *Cases Determined*, 5:468–69. During my interviews with the lawyers and judges named in the bibliography, I posed to each of them the question of why Judge Dundy did not cite Article VI of the U.S. Constitution in his decision. If he had done so, he might have been able to order the government to restore to the Poncas the land taken from them by the "clerical error" of the 1868 Treaty of Fort Laramie. All of the lawyers and judges interviewed believed that in such a case of "first impression," an unprecedented case, the judge should base his decision on a narrow interpretation of the issues presented to him and nothing more.

### 18. Standing Bear Keeps Promise

1. Tibbles, *Buckskin*, 203.

2. Tibbles, *Buckskin*, 203.

3. *Omaha Daily Herald*, May 15, 1879.

4. Jackson, *Century of Dishonor*, Appendix II. The judges of the United States Circuit Court for the Eighth Circuit for 1879–80 were identified in *Cases Determined* as: Samuel F. Miller (Supreme Court Justice assigned to the Eighth Circuit), John F. Dillon (Circuit Judge for the Eighth Circuit), and District Court judges Elmer S. Dundy (Nebraska), Cassius G. Foster (Kansas), Henry C. Caldwell (Eastern District Arkansas), Isaac C. Parker (Western District Arkansas), Moses Hallett (District of Colorado), Samuel Treat (Eastern District Missouri), James M. Love (Iowa), and Rensselaer R. Nelson (Minnesota).

5. Jackson, *Century of Dishonor*, Appendix II.

6. Jackson, *Century of Dishonor*, Appendix II.

7. *Omaha Daily Herald*, May 17, 1879.

8. Testimony of Thomas Tibbles. U.S. Congress. *Senate Select Committee Report*, 43.

9. J. Howard, *The Ponca Tribe*, 8.

10. Starita, *I Am a Man*, 176.

### 19. Gratitude and Generosity

1. Tibbles, *The Ponca Chiefs*, 112.

2. Tibbles, *The Ponca Chiefs*, 112.

3. *Omaha Daily Herald*, May 20, 1879.

4. *Omaha Daily Herald*, May 20, 1879.

5. *Omaha Daily Herald*, May 20, 1879.

6. *Omaha Daily Herald*, May 20, 1879.

7. *Omaha Daily Herald*, May 20, 1879.

8. Tibbles, *The Ponca Chiefs*, 115.

9. C. Poppleton, *The War Bonnet*, 2.

10. Tibbles, *The Ponca Chiefs*, 116.

11. C. Poppleton, *The War Bonnet*, 1–2.

12. Tibbles, *The Ponca Chiefs*, 112.

## 20. A Fire Kindled

1. Thomas Henry Tibbles Papers—Report of the Omaha Ponca Relief Committee, 1880. Smithsonian Institution, 10–11.

2. Tibbles, *Buckskin*, 205.

3. Testimony of Bright Eyes, *Senate Select Committee Report*, 26.

4. Testimony of Bright Eyes, *Senate Select Committee Report*, 27.

5. Testimony of Bright Eyes, *Senate Select Committee Report*, 27.

6. Testimony of Bright Eyes, *Senate Select Committee Report*, 32.

7. Testimony of Bright Eyes, *Senate Select Committee Report*, 32.

8. Testimony of Bright Eyes, *Senate Select Committee Report*, 33.

9. Testimony of Bright Eyes, *Senate Select Committee Report*, 35.

10. Testimony of Bright Eyes, *Senate Select Committee Report*, 35.

11. *Chicago Tribune*, May 16, 1879.

12. Tibbles, *Buckskin*, 206.

13. Tibbles, *Buckskin*, 207–11.

14. Tibbles, *Buckskin*, 213–14.

15. Tibbles, *Buckskin*, 214–15.

16. Prucha, *The Great Father*, 184. The committee consisted of Fred O. Prince (mayor of Boston), Levi C. Wade (speaker of the Massachusetts House), Henry O. Houghton (publisher), Rev. S. K. Lothrop, B. W. Williams, Henry Mason, Rev. Edward Everett Hale.

17. Tibbles, *Buckskin*, 219.

18. Tibbles, *Buckskin*, 236–39.

19. Tibbles, *The Ponca Chiefs*, 2. Dedication page. Included in the Bison Book edition of *The Ponca Chiefs* published by the University of Nebraska Press in 1972, the Note on the Text, 142, said, "*The Ponca Chiefs*, taken in conjunction with the *Daily Herald* stories, is probably as accurate an account of the basic facts of the court case as we are likely to get."

20. Tibbles, *The Ponca Chiefs*, 3.

21. Jackson's dialogue with Tibbles is found in a letter she wrote to Whitelaw Reid dated December 6, 1879, included in Mathes, *The Indian Reform Letters*, 27–28.

22. Tibbles, *Buckskin*, 296.

23. Jackson's letter to Charles Dudley Warner, December 21, 1879, included in Mathes, *The Indian Reform Letters*, 56.

## 21. Redress for Wrongs

1. The other committee members were Senators Samuel. J. Kirkwood (Iowa), P. B. Plumb (Kansas), John T. Morgan (Alabama), J. E. Bailey (Tennessee).

2. U.S. Congress, *Senate Select Committee Report*, 1, 2, 18, 19.

3. U.S. Congress, *Report of the Commission*, 1.

4. Bourke, *Diaries*, 4:232.

5. Bourke, *Diaries*, 4:232–33.

6. Bourke, *Diaries*, 4:234–35.

7. Bourke, *Diaries*, 4:235.

8. Bourke, *Diaries*, 4:237.

9. Bourke, *Diaries*, 4:255.

10. Bourke, *Diaries*, 4:255.

11. Bourke, *Diaries*, 4:256.

12. U.S. Congress, *Report of the Commission*, 5.

13. U.S. Congress, *Report of the Commission*, 6.

14. U.S. Congress, Ponca Relief Bill, 422.

15. U.S. Congress, Senate. *Report of the Secretary of the Interior*.

16. Scherer, "Dawes Act," in Wishart, *Encyclopedia*, 58–59.

## 22. Decision Sets Precedent

1. *Omaha Daily Bee*, December 4, 1880; Ponca Tribe of Indians (plaintiff) v. Makh-pi-ah-lu-tah, or Red Cloud, in his own behalf and in behalf of the Sioux Tribe of Indians (defendant).

2. *Omaha Daily Bee*, December 4, 1880. Judge Dundy's Order further decreed that "the Court does access the damages of the Plaintiff by reason of the premises at the sum of $1. It is therefore ordered by the Court that the Plaintiff recover from the Defendant the real property described in the Petition, to-wit: all the islands lying in the Niobrara River and south of the middle of the main channel of said Niobrara River and within Townships 31 and 32 North and within Ranges 6, 7, 8, 9, and 10 West of the 6th Prime Meridian of Kansas and Nebraska, and within the District and State of Nebraska."

3. Wunder and Scherer, *Echo of its Time*, 60–61. Professors John R. Wunder and Mark R. Scherer explain how Judge Dundy, a district court judge, could sit on the *Elk* case as a circuit court judge: "In 1869 congress passed 'An Act to amend the Judicial System of the United States.' This revision of the lower federal courts began the process of creating the modern appellate division, but it would take nearly forty years to straighten things out. This new structural arrangement also meant that Elmer Dundy was now for all practical purposes both the district court judge and the circuit court judge for the State of Nebraska. . . . The case was heard before the circuit court that included Judge Dundy and George Washington McCrary. . . . . McCrary served with Judge Dundy on the circuit court from 1879 to 1884. . . . The *Elk v. Wilkins* trial was heard before Judge Dundy in Omaha. Dundy kept McCrary, who remained in Iowa, posted on development." Wunder and Scherer, *Echo of Its Time*, 44–45. See also Wheeler and Harrison, *Creating the Federal Judicial System*, for a concise summary of the evolution of the history of the federal judiciary.

4. Elk v. Wilkins, 112 U.S. 94 (1884).

5. Elk v. Wilkins, 112 U.S. 94 (1884). Justice John M. Harlan, "The Great Dissenter," gave one of his first dissenting opinions in this case referring to John Elk: "If he did not acquire national citizenship on abandoning his tribe and becoming, by resident in one of the states, subject to the complete jurisdiction of the United States, then the Fourteenth Amendment has wholly failed to accomplish, in respect of the Indian race, what, we think, was intended by it; and there is still in this country a despised and rejected class of persons with no nationality whatever, who, born in our territory, owing no allegiance to any foreign power, and subject, as residents of the states, to all the burdens of government, are yet not members of any political community, nor entitled to any of the rights, privileges, or immunities of citizens of the United States." For further comments on the *Elk* decision see Lambertson, *Indian Citizenship*, 185; Bodayla, "Can an Indian Vote?," 372–80; and Lee, *Indian Citizenship and the Fourteenth Amendment*, 215–20.

6. Elk v. Wilkins, 112 U.S. 94 (1884); State *ex rel.* Bancroft v. Frear, Secretary of State, 144 Wis. 79, 128 N.W. 1068 (1910); Appeal of Leah Brunt, Administratrix, Estate of Theodore S. Brunt, United States Board of Tax Appeals, 5 B.T.A. (1926); James E. O'Neill v. Eldon Morse, 20 Mich. App. 679, 174 N.W.2d 575, (1969); Peter L. Poodry v. Tonawanda Band of Seneca Indians, 85 F.3d 874 (Ind. 1996); Dana Leigh Thompson v. County of Franklin *et al.*, 2001 WL 34355597. N.D.N.Y. (2001); Russell Means v. Navajo Nation and United States of America, 432 F.3d 924 (CA 2005); In the Matter of the Adoption of C.D.K., a Minor Child, 2009 WL 2494618 (D. Ut. 2009).

7. Cohen, *Federal Indian Law*, 177–78. Felix S. Cohen received his master's degree (1927) and PhD (1929) in philosophy from Harvard and his law degree (1931) from Columbia Law School. He was employed for fourteen years as a lawyer in the Department of the Interior and became involved in crafting President Franklin Roosevelt's Indian policy, especially the Indian Reorganization Act of 1934.

8. It is beyond the scope or purpose of this book to review federal Indian case law in the last century since the *Standing Bear* decision. For detailed analysis of this topic see Cohen, *Federal Indian Law*, and Duthu, *Indians and the Law*.

## 23. A Nation Aroused

1. Tibbles, *The Ponca Chiefs*, 3–4.

2. *Chicago Tribune*, May 13, 1879.

3. Jackson's letter to the editors of the *New York Evening Post* dated December 21, 1879, included in Mathes, *The Indian Reform Letters*, 40.

4. King, "A Better Way," 254.

5. Bourke, *Diaries*, 3:197–201.

6. Harsha, *Ploughed Under*, 1–2. *Report of the Board*, 767, supported this view: "For what ought we to hope as the future of the Indian? To this there is one answer, and but one. He should become an intelligent citizen of the United States."

7. U.S. Congress, Freedom Citizenship Suffrage Act. The United States Supreme Court's first interpretation of the Fourteenth Amendment regarding citizenship was in the *Slaughter-House* cases. *The Slaughter-House Cases*, 83 U.S. (16 Wall.) 36 (1873). The case is especially noted for a dissent given by Justice Stephen J. Field, http://www.law.cornell.edu/supremecourt/text/83/36.

8. Lake, "Standing Bear! Who?," 489.

9. Wishart, *Unspeakable Sadness*, 243.

10. Wishart, *Unspeakable Sadness*, 243. The Ponca Tribe separated into two separate entities in the late nineteenth century. Those members of the Poncas who remained in Indian Territory are known as the Southern Ponca Tribe (the "Maste-Pa-ca" or "Hot Country Poncas"), and are situated in North Central Oklahoma. Those members of the Poncas who joined Standing Bear and his initial group of twenty-nine are known as the Northern Poncas (the "Osni Pa Ca" or "Cold Country Poncas"). The government terminated the Northern Ponca Tribe in the 1960s as it had fewer than five hundred members living on about a thousand acres, reduced from the original twenty-seven thousand acres of 1890. But the desire of tribal members to preserve their unique culture and traditions for themselves and future generations led them to pursue congressional support to restore their tribal status. The Ponca Restoration Act was signed by the president in 1990. Today the official name of the tribe is "The Ponca Tribe of Nebraska," which provides health, education, social and cultural services, and resources to its members in a "Service Delivery Area" consisting of fifteen counties within Nebraska, Iowa, and South Dakota. The tribe does not have a reservation. For a good analysis of the termination and restoration of the tribal status of the Poncas, see Ritter, *The Politics of Retribalization: The Northern Ponca Case*, 237–55. *Note*: Today, Nebraska is the home of four Native American Tribes. In addition to the Northern Ponca Tribe, the Santee Sioux Tribe is headquartered in Knox County, the Winnebago Tribe in Thurston County, and the Omaha Tribe in Thurston County.

### 24. The Omaha Connection

1. Tibbles, *Buckskin*, 211–12.

2. Tibbles, *Buckskin*, 294. They were married by Rev. S. N. D. Martin.

3. Sheldon, *History and Stories*, 232. Bright Eyes illustrated a book written by her friend Fannie Reed Giffen, *Oo-Mah-Ha-Ta-Wa-Tha*. In the preface the author writes, "Most of the illustrations are the productions and reproductions of the brush and pencil of the daughter of E-sta-mah-za (Iron Eye), noted chief of the Omaha, pronounced by the tribe, Oo-mah-ha."

4. Thomas Tibbles papers can be located at the Smithsonian Institution, http://collections.si.edu/search/detail/ead_collection:sova-nmai-ac-066. *Guide to U. S. Elections* provided the following information of the Populist Party. It was organized in 1892 and held its first national convention that year in Omaha. William Jennings Bryan was its candidate in 1896 and 1900. Tibbles ran with Thomas E. Watson of Georgia in 1904 and finished fifth out of six candidates with 114,051 votes. Theo-

dore Roosevelt won the 1904 election with over 7.6 million votes. It last fielded a candidate in 1908.

5. *Omaha Sun*, August 7, 1975.

6. *Omaha Sun*, August 7, 1975.

7. Katz, *Trans-Mississippi and Internal Expositions*, 24, 93.

8. *Omaha Sun*, August 7, 1975.

9. A. Poppleton, *Reminiscences*, 34.

10. Green, *Iron Eye's Family*, xi, 97–98.

11. Wunder and Scherer, *Echo of Its Time*, 44.

12. Bourke, *On the Border* , 433.

13. Bourke, *On the Border*, 436.

14. Crook House Tour Guide.

15. Magid, *George Crook*, 7.

16. Bourke, *On the Border*, 486.

## 25. *Standing Bear at Peace*

1. Bourke, *Diaries*, 3:500; Wishart, *Encyclopedia*, 196.

2. *Cases Determined*, 5:459.

## *Acknowledgments*

1. Olson, *History of Nebraska*, 165.

2. Wolfe, *Omaha City Directory 1878–79*, 132.

3. The Omaha home addresses of the people involved in "the Omaha Connection" are: George Crook, 596 Eighteenth Street. Rev. H. D. Fisher, pastor of First Methodist Church, southside Davenport between Seventeenth and Eighteenth Streets. Rev. W. J. Harsha, pastor of Second Presbyterian Church, corner Dodge and Seventeenth Streets. Rev. E. H. Jameson, pastor of First Baptist church, southeast corner Davenport and Fifteenth Streets. Andrew J. Poppleton, attorney, 364 Dodge. Rev. A. F. Sherrill, pastor of First Congregational Church, northeast corner Chicago and Nineteenth Streets. Rev. T. Henry Tibbles, assistant editor *Omaha Herald*, northside Mason between Nineteenth and Twentieth Streets. John L. Webster, attorney, 380 Chicago Street. Wolfe, *Omaha City Directory 1878–79*.

# BIBLIOGRAPHY

*Published Works*

Abbott, Charles Greeley, ed. *Smithsonian Series 4*. New York: Smithsonian Institution, 1944 [1929].

Anderson, Grant K. "The Black Hills Exclusion Policy: Judicial Challenge." *Nebraska History* 58, no. 1 (Spring 1977): 1–24.

*Black's Law Dictionary*. 6th ed. St. Paul: West, 1990.

Blackstone, William. *Commentaries on the Laws of England*. Edited by W. M. Hardcastle Browne. St. Paul: West, 1897 [1750].

Bodayla, Stephen D. "Can an Indian Vote?: *Elk v. Wilkins*: A Setback for Indian Citizenship." *Nebraska History* 67, no. 4 (Winter 1986): 372–80.

Bourke, John G. *Diaries 3: June 1, 1875–June 22, 1880*. Edited by Charles M. Robinson III. Denton: University of North Texas Press, 2007.

———. *Diaries 4: July 3, 1880–May 22, 1881*. Edited by Charles M. Robinson III. Denton: University of North Texas Press, 2009.

———. *On the Border with Crook*. Lincoln: University of Nebraska Press, 1971.

Brown, Wallace. "George L. Miller and the Boosting of Omaha." *Nebraska History* 50, no. 3 (Fall 1969): 277–91.

Capps, Benjamin. *The Old West: The Indians*. New York: Time-Life, 1973.

Carlson, Paul H. *The Plains Indians*. College Station: Texas A&M University Press, 1998.

*Cases Determined in the United States, Circuit Courts for the Eighth Circuit. 5*. Reported by John F. Dillon, the Circuit Judge. Davenport IA: Egbert, Fidlar & Chambers, 1880.

Catlin, George. *Letters and Notes on the Manners, Customs and Conditions of North American Indians, vol. 1*. New York: Dover, 1973.

Cohen, Felix S. *Handbook of Federal Indian Law: With Reference Tables and Index*. Washington DC: Government Printing Office, 1942.

Dando-Collins, Stephen. *Standing Bear Is a Person*. Cambridge MA: DaCapo, 2004.

Danziger, Danny, and John Gillingham. *1215: The Year of Magna Carta*. New York: Simon & Schuster-Touchstone, 2005.

DeMallie, Raymond J. "The Buffalo: The First Voices." *Nebraskaland Magazine* 62, no. 1 (January-February 1984): 60–61. Nebraska Game and Parks Commission.

Dorsey, James Owen. "Migrations of Siouan Tribes." *American Naturalist* 20, no. 30 (March 1886): 211–22.

Douglas County Historical Society. *The Banner* (Omaha NE). December 2008.

———. *General Crook House Museum Tour Guide*. Omaha. 2018.

Duthu, N. Bruce. *American Indians and the Law*. New York: Viking Penguin, 2008.

Fletcher, Alice C., and Francis LaFlesche. *The Omaha Tribe, vol. 1*. Lincoln: University of Nebraska Press, 1992. (Originally published by Smithsonian Institution Bureau of American Ethnology [Washington DC: Government Printing Office, 1911].)

——. *The Omaha Tribe, vol. 2*. Lincoln: University of Nebraska Press, 1992. (Originally published by Smithsonian Institution Bureau of American Ethnology [Washington DC: Government Printing Office, 1911].)

Fort Omaha Walking Tour. Omaha: Metropolitan Community College. http://www.mccneb.edu.Fort-Omaha-Campus-History.

Giffen, Fannie Reed. *Oo-Mah-Ha-Ta-Wa-Tha*. Lincoln NE: Self-published, 1898.

Green, Norma Kidd. *Iron Eye's Family: The Children of Joseph LaFlesche*. Lincoln: Nebraska State Historical Society, 1969.

Habeas Corpus Act of 1679. Parliament of England Statute of 31 Car. II, C.2.

Harsha, William. *Ploughed Under: The Story of an Indian Chief*. New York: Fords, Howard & Hulbert, 1881.

Hoig, Stan. *White Man's Paper Trail: Grand Councils and Treaty-Making on the Central Plains*. Boulder: University Press of Colorado, 2006.

Howard, James H. *The Ponca Tribe*. Lincoln: University of Nebraska Press, 1995. Originally published by the Smithsonian Institution Bureau of American Ethnology, Bulletin no. 195 (Washington: U.S. GPO, 1965).

*In the Matter of the Application of Ma-chu-nah-zha (Standing Bear), et al., for a Writ of Habeas Corpus*. Omaha: Douglas County Historical Society Archives.

Jackson, Helen Hunt. *A Century of Dishonor: A Sketch of the United States Government's Dealings with Some of the Indian Tribes*. Boston 1885. Project Gutenberg, 2015. www.gutenberg.org.

Katz, Wendy Jean, ed. *The Trans-Mississippi and International Expositions of 1898–1899*. Lincoln: University of Nebraska Press, 2018.

King, James T. "A Better Way: General George Crook and the Ponca Indians." *Nebraska History 50* (Fall 1969): 239–56.

Lake, James A., Sr. "Standing Bear! Who?." *Nebraska Law Review* 60, no. 3 (1981): 451–503.

Lambertson, Genio M. "Indian Citizenship." *American Law Review* 20 (March-April 1886): 183–85.

Larsen, Lawrence H., and Barbara J. Cottrell. *The Gate City: A History of Omaha*. Lincoln: University of Nebraska Press, 1997.

Lee, R. Anton. *Indian Citizenship and the Fourteenth Amendment*. Pierre: South Dakota State Historical Society, 1974.

Magid, Paul. *George Crook: From the Redwoods to Appomattox*. Norman: University of Oklahoma Press, 2011.

Mathes, Valerie Sherer, ed. *The Indian Reform Letters of Helen Hunt Jackson, 1879–1885*. Norman: University of Oklahoma Press, 1998.

Mathes, Valerie Sherer, and Richard Lowitt. *The Standing Bear Controversy: Prelude to Indian Reform*. Chicago: University of Illinois Press, 2003.

Miller, Perry. *Roger Williams: His Contribution to the American Tradition*. New York: Atheneum, 1965.

Moulton, Gary E., ed. *The Definitive Journals of Lewis & Clark: Vol. 3 of the Nebraska Edition*. Lincoln: University of Nebraska Press, 1987.

Nichols, Roger L. *General Henry Atkinson*. Norman: University of Oklahoma Press, 1965.

Olson, James C. *History of Nebraska*. Lincoln: University of Nebraska Press, 1974.

Ordinance for the Government of the Territory of United States Northwest of the River Ohio. https://www.ourdocuments.gov/doc.php?flash=false&doc=8&page =Transcript.

Phillips, George H. *The Indian Ring in Dakota Territory, 1870-1890*. Pierre: South Dakota State Historical Society, 1972.

Poppleton, Andrew J. *Reminiscences*. Lincoln: Nebraska Historical Society, 1915.

Poppleton, Caroline L. *The War Bonnet*. Lincoln: Nebraska Historical Society, 1915.

Porter, Joseph C. *Paper Medicine Man: John Gregory Bourke and His American West*. Norman: University of Oklahoma Press, 1986.

Prucha, Francis Paul. *The Great Father*. Lincoln: University of Nebraska Press, 1996.

Reilly, Hugh J. *Bound to Have Blood: Frontier Newspapers and the Plains Indian Wars*. Lincoln: University of Nebraska Press, 2011.

Remini, Robert V. *The Life of Andrew Jackson*. New York: Penguin, HarperCollins, 1990.

*Reply of the Boston Committee to Secretary of Interior Carl Schurz*. Boston: Frank Wood, 1881.

Ritter, Beth R. "Piecing Together the Ponca Past: Reconstructing Degiha Migrations to the Great Plains." *Great Plains Quarterly* 2307 (Fall 2002): 271-84.

———. "The Politics of Retribalization: The Northern Ponca Case." *Great Plains Quarterly* 233 (August 1994): 237-55.

Schach, Paul. "Maximilian, Prince of Wied (1782-1867): Reconsidered." *Great Plains Quarterly* 14, no. 1 (Winter 1994): 5-20. http://digitalcommons.unl.edu. /greatplainsquarterly/853.

Sheldon, Addison E. *History and Stories of Nebraska*. Lincoln: University Publishing, 1926.

Snoddy, Don, Barry Combes, Bob Marks, and Del Weber, eds. *Their Man in Omaha. The Barker Letters:1, 1860-1868*. Omaha: Douglas County Historical Society, 2004.

Starita, Joe. *I Am a Man*. New York: St. Martin's, 2009.

Tibbles, Thomas H. *Buckskin and Blanket Days*. Lincoln: University of Nebraska Press, 1969.

Tibbles, Thomas H. *The Ponca Chiefs: An Account of the Trial of Standing Bear*. Edited by Kay Graber. Lincoln: University of Nebraska Press, 1972 [1880].

———. Thomas Tibbles Papers. Smithsonian Institution. National Museum of the American Indian Archives Center. http://collections.si.edu/search/detail/ead _collection:sova-nmai-ac-066.

Tocqueville, Alexis de. *Democracy in America*. 1835. Edited by Richard D. Heffner. New York: New American Library, 1956.

U.S. Congress. General Allotment Act of 1887 (Dawes Act). 24 Stat. 388. Ch 119, 25 USCA 331. 49th Cong. 2d Sess.

———. Habeas Corpus Act of 1867. 14 Stat. 385.

———. Habeas Corpus Suspension Act of 1863. 12 Stat. 755.

———. Homestead Act of 1862. Pub L. 37–64.

———. Indian Appropriation Act of 1871. 16 Stat. 566. 41st Cong. 3d Sess.

———. Indian Freedom Citizenship Suffrage Act of 1924 (Snyder Act). 8 U.S.C. ch. 12, subch. 111, 1041b. 68th Cong. 1st Sess. https://legislink.org/us/stat.

———. Indian Removal Act of 1830. 21st Cong. 1st Sess., Ch. 148.

———. Judiciary Act of 1789. 1 Stat. 73 (Codified in Title 28 of the U.S.C.A.).

———. Kansas-Nebraska Act of 1854. 10 Stat. 277. 33rd Cong.

———. Ponca Relief Bill of 1881. 21 Stat. 422. 49th Cong.

———. Ponca Restoration Act of 1990. Pub L. No. 101-484. 5,104 Stat. 1167. 101st Cong.

———. *Report of the Board of Indian Commissioners.* H.R. Exec. Doc. No. 1, 49th Cong. 1st Sess. 1881.

U.S. Congress. Senate. *A Report of the Commission Appointed December 18, 1880, to Ascertain the Facts in Regard to the Removal of the Ponca Indians* (the Ponca Commission). Select Comm. Ex. Doc. No. 30. 46th Cong. 3d Sess. 1881.

———. *Report of the Committee on the Judiciary.* 41st Cong. 3d Sess. no. 268. Washington DC: Government Printing Office. 1870.

———. *Report of the Secretary of the Interior.* H.R. Ex. Doc. No. 1. 47th Cong. 1st Sess. 1881.

———. *Report of the Senate Select Committee on Removal of Northern Cheyennes as to the Removal and Situation of the Ponca Indians.* Report No. 670, 46th Cong. 2d Sess. 1880.

———. *Testimony Before the Select Committee on Removal of Northern Cheyennes as to the Removal and Situation of the Ponca Indians.* Mis Doc. No. 49. 46th Cong. 3d Sess. 1881.

U.S. Constitution. *Black's Law Dictionary.* 6th ed. St. Paul: West, 1990.

U.S. Department of the Interior. *Annual Report of the Secretary of the Interior for 1877.* Journal of March. E. A. Howard. Washington DC: Government Printing Office, 1877.

———. *Annual Report of the Secretary of the Interior for 1878.* Washington DC: Government Printing Office, 1878.

———. *Annual Report of the Secretary of the Interior for 1879.* Washington DC: Government Printing Office, 1879.

U.S. Department of the Interior, Office of Indian Affairs. *Annual Report of the Commissioner of Indian Affairs for 1858.* Washington DC: Government Printing Office, 1858.

———. Letter of E. A. Brooks, Acting Commissioner, to G. M. Lambertson, U.S. District Attorney, April 22, 1879 (Ponca, L. 358, 1879).

U.S. Office of the *Federal Register* and *Congressional Quarterly*'s *Guide to U.S. Elections.* 4th ed. 2001.

U.S.-Ponca Treaty of 1817. http://www.firstpeople.us/FP-Html-Treaties/Treaties.html.

U.S.-Ponca Treaty of 1825. http://www.firstpeople.us/FP-Html-Treaties/Treaties.html.

U.S.-Ponca Treaty of 1858. http://www.firstpeople.us/FP-Html-Treaties/Treaties.html.

U.S.-Ponca Treaty of 1865. http://www.firstpeople.us/FP-Html-Treaties/Treaties.html.

U.S.-Sioux Brule Treaty of 1868. http://www.firstpeople.us/FP-Html-Treaties/Treaties.html.

Utley, Robert M. *The Indian Frontier of the American West 1846–1890*. Albuquerque: University of New Mexico Press, 1984.

Watson, Blake A. *Buying America from the Indians:* Johnson v. McIntosh *and the History of Native Land Rights*. Norman: University of Oklahoma Press, 2012.

Wheeler, Russell R., and Cynthia Harrison. *Creating The Federal Judicial System*. 3rd ed. Federal Judicial Center, 2005.

Wilson, D. Ray. *Nebraska Historical Tour Guide*. Carpentersville IL: Crossroads, 1983.

Wishart, David J., ed. *Encyclopedia of the Great Plains Indians*. Lincoln: University of Nebraska Press, 2007.

———. *An Unspeakable Sadness: The Dispossession of the Nebraska Indians*. Lincoln: University of Nebraska Press, 1994.

Wolfe, J. M. *Omaha City Directory 1878–79*. Omaha: Herald Publishing.

Worcester, Donald E. "The Friends of the Indian and the Peace Policy." In *Forked Tongues and Broken Treaties*, 254–91. Edited by Donald E. Worcester. Caldwell ID: Caxton, 1975.

Wright, Charles E. *Law at Little Big Horn*. Lubbock: Texas Tech University Press, 2016.

Wunder, John R., and Mark R. Scherer. *Echo of Its Time: The History of the Federal District Court of Nebraska, 1867–1933*. Lincoln: University of Nebraska Press, 2019.

*Judicial Decisions*

Appeal of Leah Brunt, Administratrix, Estate of Theodore S. Brunt, United States Board of Tax Appeals, 5 B.T.A. (1926).

The Cherokee Nation v. The State of Georgia, 30 U.S. 1 (1831).

Dana Leigh Thompson v. County of Franklin et al, 2001 WL 34355597. (N.D.N.Y. 2001).

Dred Scott v. Sandford, 60 U.S. 393 (1857)

Elk v. Wilkins, 112 U.S. 94 (1884).

*Ex parte* Merryman, 17 F. Cas. 144. (Md. 1861).

Fay v. Noia, 372 U.S. 391, 401–02 (1963).

In the Matter of the Adoption of C.D.K., a Minor Child, 2009 WL 2494618 (D. Ut. 2009)

James E. O'Neill v. Eldon Morse, 20 Mich. App. 679, 174 N.W.2d 575 (1969).

Johnson and Graham's Lessee v. William M'Intosh, 21 U.S. 543 (1823).

Kidd v. Norman, 651 F. 3d 947 (8th Cir. 2011).

Peter L. Poodry v. Tonawanda Band of Seneca Indians, 85 F.3d 874 (Ind. 1996).

Peyton v. Rowe, 391 U.S. 54 (1968).

Ponca Tribe of Indians v. Makh-pi-ah-lu-tah, or Red Cloud, in his own behalf and in behalf of the Sioux Tribe of Indians. Fed. Dist. Ct. (D. Nebraska 1880).

Preiser v. Rodriguez, 411 U.S. 475 (1973).

Russell Means v. Navajo Nation and United States of America, 432 F.3d 924 (Cal. 2005).

Slaughter House Cases, 83 U.S. (16 Wall.) 36 (1873).

Smith v. O'Grady, 313 U.S. 329 (1941).

State v. Central Lumber Co. 123 N.W. 504 (S.D. 1909).

State *ex rel.* Bancroft v. Frear, Secretary of State, 144 Wis. 79, 128 N.W. 1068 (1910).

United States v. Schooner Peggy, 5 U.S. 103, 109–110, 2 L.Ed. 49 (1801).

United States v. Sioux Nation of Indians, 448 U.S. 371 (1980).

United States *ex rel.* Standing Bear v. Crook, 5 Dil. 453, 25 F. Cas. 695 (D. Nebraska 1879).

*Interviews*

The following distinguished individuals graciously gave of their time and expertise to meet with the author at various times between 2009 and 2019 (position at time of interview).

Harold Anderson: retired publisher and chief executive officer of the *Omaha World Herald*; lecturer on General Crook and the trial of Standing Bear.

Hon. Laurie Smith Camp: chief judge of U.S. District Court for the District of Nebraska.

Betty Davis: executive director, Douglas County Historical Society, Crook House at Fort Omaha.

Judi M. gaiashkibos: executive director, Nebraska Commission on Indian Affairs, member Ponca Tribe.

Hon. Thomas K. Harmon: judge, Douglas County Court.

Teresa A. Trumbly Lamsam, PhD: professor emeritus, University of Nebraska–Omaha, member Osage Tribe.

John P. Mullen, JD: attorney, Fellow of the American College of Trial Lawyers.

Charles E. Wright, JD: author, retired attorney, Cline, Williams, Wright, Johnson & Oldfather.

# INDEX

Printed in the USA
CPSIA information can be obtained
at www.ICGtesting.com
CBHW030841160424
6934CB00003B/20